CAROL VORDERMAN'S **30-DAY**
CELLULITE PLAN

Fight cellulite, lose weight, feel great

With Anita Bean, Linda Bird and Sarah Williams

ACKNOWLEDGEMENTS

Virgin Books Ltd would like to thank all those women who took part in the trials for this book, without whose help and enthusiasm it would not have been possible.

First published in Great Britain in 2004 by
Virgin Books Ltd, Thames Wharf Studios, Rainville Road, London W6 9HA

Copyright © Carol Vorderman 2004

The right of Carol Vorderman to be identified as the author of this work has been asserted by her in accordance with the Copyright, Designs and Patents Act 1988.

A catalogue record for this book is available from the British Library.

ISBN 0 7535 1095 2

This edition produced for The Book People
Hall Wood Avenue, Haydock, St Helens WA11 9UL

All photographs by Karl Grant
Designed and typeset by Smith & Gilmour

Printed and bound by Bath Press, CPI Group

CHECK WITH YOUR DOCTOR

Before starting this or any other diet programme, you should consult your doctor. In particular, this should be done with regard to any allergies you may have to the foods, drinks, products or other recommendations contained in this programme. The diet and exercises may not be suitable for everyone. Pregnant women should be especially careful and ensure that their doctor advises that the diet and exercises are suitable for them. If you are taking medication or have any medical condition, you should check with your doctor first.

While the authors have made every effort to ensure that the information contained in this book is as accurate as possible, it is advisory only and should not be used as an alternative to seeking specialist medical advice. The authors and publishers cannot be held responsible for actions that may be taken by a reader as a result of reliance on the information contained in this book, which are taken entirely at the reader's own risk.

Carol Vorderman was assisted in the writing of this book by:

Anita Bean BSc, an award-winning nutritionist and the author of 12 books, including Carol Vorderman's Detox for Life series. She writes for numerous magazines and newspapers and is also a broadcaster on TV and radio.

Linda Bird, a former Deputy Editor of *Zest* magazine and Senior Editor of *She* magazine, and a freelance writer on health and wellbeing.

Sarah Williams, who is a personal trainer with many celebrities on her client list and who has advised numerous magazines on fitness and exercise.

Contents

INTRODUCTION

Girls, we all know IT exists. Even if you try your best to ignore IT and pretend it isn't there. Somehow, when you catch yourself in a brightly lit mirror, you know that those ridges and bumps just haven't gone away. IT is of course…

CELLULITE!!!!!!!!!
Aargh!!! Ugh!! Bleeergh!

Cellulite is the scourge of more or less every woman over the age of 25. It can be found smiling contentedly from the bottoms of women who are slim, women who are overweight, mothers, single girls, fit women and couch potatoes. However, just as with many other things in life, men seem to have been drinking from the lucky cup. They shop in the NO CELLULITE R US stores. Even if they have bellies the size of a pregnant elephant, there isn't even an inkling of orange peel to be found. Not a whiff. Not fair perhaps, but true, and sadly for the other half of the human race (that's us), there are pre-programmed, hormone related, biological reasons for the difference.

Have you looked at yourself under a bit of harsh lighting, or caught a bad and bumpy reflection in a changing-room mirror recently? As the years have gone by, have you noticed saggy skin starting to creep around your belly and the backs of your arms? Do you notice when you're sitting down that lumps appear at the tops of your thighs, and your skin turns to orange peel? Some of you might be whispering 'yes' and others might be screaming out the same answer. If you are, then this is definitely the plan for you.

With the 30-Day Cellulite Plan, you will find the following differences:
You'll lose weight. Our testers lost up to 10lbs in 30 days, but I know of many others who have followed my detox diet who have lost up to one and a half stones in the same number of days. The amount will merely depend on how strictly you follow the diet.
Your skin will feel fantastic. You will see a huge difference in your skin all over your face and body.
Your cellulite will improve dramatically. Just look at the before and after pictures of our testers on the cover and inside the book to see the kind of result that you could also achieve.
You'll have bundles of energy. Because of the diet and the fact that you will have been exercising, your energy levels will increase dramatically making you feel better and younger than you have for years.

Over the years I've been afflicted with cellulite, sometimes really badly. I first noticed the deviant dimples when I was 26. Well, to be more precise, it was noticed for me. I was sitting in a bar in Leeds with some preposterous 80s mini skirt on, legs crossed and having a good laugh with my girlfriends when a bloke at the bar (who'd asked me out the week before, but I'd said no on account of his matching bad breath and hair) shouted, 'Ooh Carol, you've got lumps on your legs. Is that cellulite?' Well, hell hath no fury like a pea-brained bloke scorned, I suppose, and he'd got his revenge good and proper. Was I embarrassed? Oh yes, big time. I wished the ground could swallow me up and deposit me at the other end of the M62. Unfortunately, the ground swallowing wasn't happening that night and I eventually had to be escorted out surrounded on all sides by my mates just so that IT couldn't be seen again. Needless to say, I signed up with a gym the very next day and tried to sweat it all off in a Jane Fonda workout way ('going for the burn' was very big in the 80s).

The exercise did reduce it (and the gym fees reduced my bank balance), but the cellulite never went completely. Of course, back in those days the medical profession refused to accept that cellulite existed and, consequently, there weren't any products or self-help books specifically targeting the problem. If I knew then what I know now, I could have solved it completely within a month and then worn hot pants all summer just to prove a point. But I never did have a chance to grab back any points against the Ugly Bloke. He won that battle. Oh, the joys of youth. Not.

Nowadays, of course, these public showdowns come thick and fast courtesy of photos in magazines and newspapers. How great it makes us all feel when some celeb is caught with her cellulite bumps on show. To be perfectly honest, it terrifies the life out of me when I go on holiday. The thought of getting caught without make-up and virtually naked in your mid forties in the glare of the midday sun is not a pleasant one. But it goes with the job, and I'm not complaining…yet.

But it's the same for many of us. Whenever you're out on the beach, or at the pool, you only have to look around at women over the age of 25 to see that cellulite can afflict different shapes and sizes of women. It also seems to increase with age and the number of children you bear and we'll explain why in one of our chapters. I've experienced it first hand.

Since my humiliation at the hands of the Prize Pillock in Leeds my weight has fluctuated tremendously. I've given birth twice, and with all the bad eating habits my body's had to endure over the years the cellulite just got worse and worse. At my heaviest I was more than 2 stones overweight and three dress sizes larger than I am now. The cellulite had found a permanent home on my backside and legs until I first discovered the Detox diet (more details of the Detox for Life book range are on page.143). On my first 28-day session of detoxing I changed what I ate completely. I replaced processed ready meals, caffeine drinks, wheat and dairy with fresh fruit and veg, mineral- and vitamin-rich foods, water and healthy living. The fat dropped off and the bumps seemed to melt away. I would estimate that in that short space of time I lost a dress size and a half, and with it about three quarters of the cellulite. And yet, when I had been that weight years before, the cellulite was still there. So what had made the difference to my before and after situation? The difference was WHAT I had eaten, not how many calories I'd been taking in. I knew then that the effects of a detox diet were very different to those of any calorie-counting or protein-rich diet. The weight loss on the Detox diet was just as good (if not better in many cases), but the energy and the difference in my skin was excellent.

Since then, many creams and potions have come on to the market to combat cellulite and salon treatments have become popular. But I strongly believe that without changing your diet and doing a bit of exercise you will never get rid of cellulite completely or permanently.

With all of this experience in my own life and having received tens of thousands of e-mails from detoxers, I decided to get together with experts in the fields of nutrition, beauty and exercise to come up with this 30-Day Cellulite Plan.

We wanted something which could help you to lose weight and say goodbye to orange peel legs, dimpled bums and bingo wings. With our combined knowledge and experience we came up the plan in this book. It's very easy to write a plan with what you think is going to be good advice, but the proof of how good any plan is comes only when it's tested for real.

So we needed to try it out. Funnily enough it was easy to find women who'd been blighted with cellulite for years and wanted to get rid of it and who didn't mind having photos taken of their bottoms (how brave are they?). Women in their twenties, thirties, forties, fifties and sixties all came forward. And what brilliant testers they have been. The before and after photos show just how good the plan is. You can see how the ridges, bumps and inches have disappeared for good. Some of the girls now want to carry on with the plan to get rid of even more weight and bumps and I wish them all the best of luck. I know that with extra time their figures will continue to get better and better.

So what about you and your secret wishes? What is it that you want to do? How much weight do you realistically want to lose? While you're reading through this book, keep looking at the before and after pics for inspiration.

HOW TO USE THIS BOOK

You're going to need to read through the book completely before you start, so that you understand what cellulite is and what causes it (these are explained in the first two chapters) and then the plan itself, which will tell you all about the diet and the exercise routine that is involved. Following the plan, you will find details of the recipes and the instructions for the exercises, as well as chapters on treatments you can do at home or have at a salon. Some of our testers tried creams or salon treatments while they completed the plan, but if you can't afford them, don't worry. You will still achieve a great difference.

Everything in this book has been designed to make the 30-Day Plan as simple as possible for you, and with minimal expense. The exercise plan has been designed so that you don't need to pay for a gym membership, but you will need some small weights. And to make it easy, I particularly wanted tick boxes on the pages of the 30-Day Plan, which have been put right next to all the things you are going to have to do that day. Think good things about yourself and you'll tackle the next day with more energy.

I have always found that drinking water is the key to a good detox plan. I really want you to drink as much water as you can and to help, here are my mini rules for water.

• We have recommended a minimum of 2 litres of water a day. I prefer to drink 3–4 litres when I'm on a detox as the benefits are many and marvellous.
• Drink tap water if you don't want to fork out for bottled water.
• Drink your water at room temperature or slightly warm. It's much easier to drink at room temperature.
• Keep a very large tumbler in the bathroom and drink almost a litre of water while you're getting ready in the morning.
• Have a very large tumbler of water 5–10 minutes before every meal. It will reduce your hunger dramatically.
• Remember the more water you drink, the less you will feel the urge to drink booze or coffee.

So drink the water, do the exercises, tick the boxes and when it's time to go to bed, just look at what you've achieved and be proud of yourself. You're doing well and, remember: if you complete the plan, then fantastic results should be yours. You, too, will have your very own before and after.

Go girl!!!

Carol Vorderman

CHAPTER 1
WHAT IS CELLULITE?

Ask women which parts of their body they're least happy with and the chances are they'll nominate their bottom and their thighs.

Many of us, particularly pear-shaped women – the traditional English bodyshape – tend to gain weight on those areas. In fact these bits often remain flabby even when we successfully manage to lose weight elsewhere. But it's not just the size of our thighs that troubles us. It's the texture of our skin.

How do you describe yours? Smooth as a baby's bottom or more like a big squishy sponge? Some refer to those dimply, wobbly, fatty areas as 'orange peely'; to others, it's like 'cottage cheese'. Often the skin is red and blotchy, too – it can even be painful to the touch. Occasionally, women also find this kind of puckered skin on their arms and stomach. And if statistics are anything to go by at least 80–90 per cent of us have some form of it somewhere on our bodies!

We're talking, of course, about the dreaded cellulite. It unites women of all ages and body shapes, too; only a very lucky few go through life without it.

Some women notice it gets worse when they gain pounds; others find it's more noticeable if they lose a lot of weight in a short space of time. It may increase after childbirth – or when you reach the menopause.

Sometimes you only really notice you've got cellulite when you cross your legs. It can come as a nasty shock – especially if your bottom and thighs appear wonderfully smooth and even textured when you stand up in front of the mirror. But have you noticed, when you sit down or squeeze your thighs between your fingers you see, to your dismay, a handful of lumps and bumps?

Cellulite seems to affect even the slimmest, most beautiful actresses and models too. The tabloids and glossy magazines are always publishing unflattering pictures of the orange-peely behinds of otherwise perfectly formed celebrities. And countless column inches are devoted to various treatments for it, from 'anti-cellulite' garments to the latest lotions, potions and 'miracle' food supplements.

Perhaps we should start by establishing what cellulite *is* exactly?

The truth is, many of us would be forgiven for thinking it is some kind of stubborn, mysterious skin condition.

The name cellulite was first coined back in the 70s, but the 'condition' was discussed by European scientists as early as the 19th century. Until recently it baffled everyone. Over the years all sorts of culprits have been held responsible for cellulite – namely 'toxins'. Everything from smoking and drinking alcohol to caffeine, even pesticides in our food and drink, have been blamed for the 'abnormal' tissue on our bottoms.

But there's nothing particularly abnormal about it. The truth is – wait for it – cellulite is just fat, according to dermatologists. Specifically, it's subcutaneous fat, the top layer of fat just beneath our skin. We know this now, because when this kind of skin was analysed by scientists from the Laboratory of Human Behaviour and Metabolism at Rockerfeller University in New York in 1998, it was found to be no different from subcutaneous fat found elsewhere on the body.

So what makes it look different? Experts say that it comes down to the tissue that holds the fat in place in these areas – the bottom, thighs, tummy and arms.

Think of the fat that covers your body as being separated into lots of little boxes made up of collagen fibres (known as *septae*). These collagen fibres basically keep your fat in place. Now imagine what happens when you gain weight: the fat cells inside the little boxes swell and effectively cause the fat to bulge out of each little box – a bit like a loaf of bread swells up and out of the tin when it's baked, or sausage meat oozes out of its skin when it's cooked. And that's effectively what you see on your thighs – lots and lots of little pointy, domed shaped dimples as the fat squishes out of its little fat box.

So why doesn't this squishy fat business affect men? Basically, because the type of connective tissue holding the fat boxes in place is slightly different in men. In men, the collagen fibres run diagonally, which hold the fat down. In women, it runs horizontally, so there's nothing to stop the fat from bulging and puckering out over the top. Also, female hormones are responsible for the distribution of fat over our bottoms, thighs and stomachs, which may explain why we get more cellulite in these areas than elsewhere on our body.

Of course, the laying down of cellulite involves more than just fat, otherwise why would slim women get it too?

Experts say that water retention also plays a part in the dimpling appearance of skin on bottoms and thighs. One study published in the *International Journal of Dermatology* found that cellulite has more water-attracting cells than elsewhere on the body. So as your body retains water, the fat cells expand more and stretch the connective tissue – and the result is bulging fat cells beneath our skin, which give cellulite that bumpy appearance. (We'll look at water retention and why it may happen in the next chapter.)

Other factors are involved in cellulite, too. As we age, or as our skin's tissues are damaged by a lack of oxygen (perhaps because of a sedentary lifestyle, or bad circulation), the connective tissues become tougher and less elastic and flexible. So, while the surrounding tissue continues to expand with surplus weight, or water gain, the toughened fibres pull down and make those fatty bulges look even more dimpled and puckered.

And that's it really: cellulite is the appearance of overstuffed fatty cells underneath the skin, swollen by water or too much fat, and held in place by fibres which may have lost their elasticity. As a result the fat bulges out over the top. We'll look at some of the reasons why this may happen to *your* bottom and thighs in the next chapter.

The cellulite test. What can you see?

Now, though, it's time to take a look at yourself in the mirror.

How bad is your cellulite?

Once you assess the extent of the problem, you can begin to address it in a realistic way.

Obviously, if you have the kind of widespread cellulite that you can see through some pairs of flimsy trousers, then you have your work cut out for you, as it certainly isn't going to disappear overnight. But don't despair; there's plenty that you can do nowadays to get smoother thighs in weeks. The 30-day programme in this book has been specifically designed to help reduce the appearance of cellulite by following a cleansing diet and an exercise routine which targets the areas most affected and backed up by skin brushing and complemented by the use of a treatment of your choice that you can do at home. Later on, we also look at salon treatments which you may also wish to include in your programme, but which don't form part of the basic programme.

According to experts, cellulite can be classified into four stages. This is based upon its appearance while you're standing, or lying, or pinching the skin.

Try it now. Make sure you have plenty of (ideally, natural) light while you're doing this test.

Stage 1: Your thighs, bottom and stomach look smooth when you stand up or lie down. And when you do the pinch test you just see folds of skin, not dimples. Lucky you.

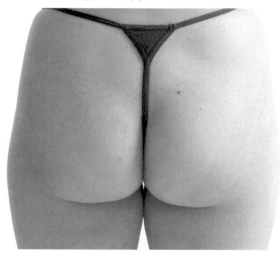

Stage 2: When you stand or are lying down, the skin looks nice and smooth. But when you do the pinch test you can see dimples and fatty pockets.

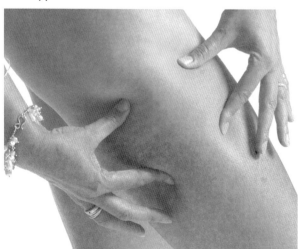

Stage 3: Your skin is still smooth when you're lying down, but when you're standing up, you can see pitting, bulging and unevenness in your skin.

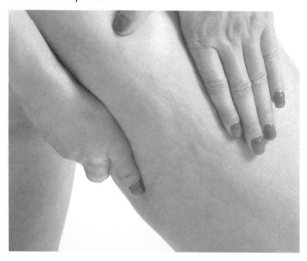

Stage 4: You can see the dimples and puckering clearly whether you pinch or not and no matter whether you're lying down or standing up. It can be pretty widespread – appearing on your hips, thighs, bottom and stomach. It may even be painful to the touch.

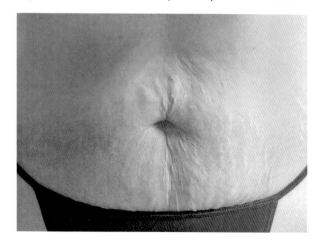

How did it go? If you're a stage 4, don't despair. Help is at hand!

CHAPTER 2
WHAT CAUSES CELLULITE?

Cellulite has always been a bit of a mystery to skin experts and beauty gurus. Everyone has his or her own theory about what it *is*, and what may cause it. As a result, the routes to a cellulite-free behind have always been many – or controversial.

In recent years, although experts may have discovered more about the anatomy of cellulite, the jury is still out on what, definitively, *causes* it. Here, we are going to look at some of the possible culprits behind that dreaded orange-peel skin. Once we understand our enemy – or potential enemies – it's so much easier to fight them!

Take a look at the following and ask yourself which may be causing your own cellulite.

1 You're all woman?

OK, you're female, and there's not much you can do about that. Studies show that men, by virtue of their testosterone, very rarely develop cellulite. That's because they have more muscle and less fat than women, and their fat tends to be laid down in their abdominal area rather than their hips and thighs. Their outer skin is thicker so their subcutaneous fat is less noticeable. Testosterone is responsible for men's stronger, firmer connective fibres. In women, the collagen is weaker, so the fat boxes under the skin don't stand so squarely.

Oestrogen is a prime culprit because it encourages fluid retention, which causes women's fat cells to bulge out. Some experts have found that women notice their cellulite is worse when they're taking the contraceptive pill. It can also get worse during or after pregnancy when your hormone levels surge. That may be because body fat produces more oestrogen, so the more body fat you have, the more oestrogen you produce. Aiming to keep your weight down with a low-fat diet and regular exercise is one way to keep control of your oestrogen levels.

2 Is your mother to blame?

And her mother, and her mother before her? Experts say the predisposition to cellulite seems to be genetically inherited. Some women simply have more fat cells, poorer circulation, weaker veins, less powerful lymphatic vessels, or are more 'hormonally sensitive' than others. To a large extent you have inherited your mother's skin type and genetic make up – so if she has thin skin and poor circulation, which tends to make cellulite worse, then there's a chance yours will be too. You may also have inherited your mother's metabolic rate, or eating habits – or at least learned them from her – which may make you more prone to weight gain.

3 Are you overweight?

Here's something that's more within your control – despite your genetic inheritance. When you gain weight, you effectively increase the number of fat cells under the skin and, as we explained in chapter one, when you lay down fat, it tends to bulge out between the fibres of connective tissue, causing that bumpy, dimpled appearance.

So, the first step is to determine whether or not you are overweight. You probably know the answer to this question, but do the tests below to assess the problem. In the UK, nearly two-thirds of men and over half of all women are now overweight – and one in five are obese (that is, they are at least 2–3 stones overweight). The level of obesity has tripled in the past twenty years and is still rising. At this rate, by 2010 at least one in four adults will be obese.

These statistics are alarming because being overweight, and especially being obese, increases our risk of many health problems. Cellulite is just one tiny side-effect. Other, more serious effects include Type 2 diabetes, heart disease, certain cancers, stroke, back and joint pain, osteoarthritis, infertility, breathlessness, depression, snoring and difficulty sleeping – to mention a few.

Quite simply, being obese or overweight can stop you getting the best from life. In fact, a high profile report from the National Audit Office concluded that obesity could shave an average of nine years from our life span. If a desire to get rid of cellulite spurs you to lose weight, so much the better; you'll gain a hundredfold. Right – now's time for a self-assessment. If you're worried about your weight, see your GP. If you're a member of a gym, you can ask them to measure your fat using callipers.

Basically, if you're taking in more calories than you're expending, you're going to get fat, and be more prone to cellulite. Start by trying to work out how many calories your body actually needs per day; you can do the maths yourself.

Try the following two sums. The first helps you work out your body mass index (BMI).

1) Your BMI = your weight in kilogrammes divided by your height in metres squared.
For example, if you weigh 10 st 4 lb (65 g) and are 5 ft 4 in (1.62m), then 65 divided by (1.62 x 1.62) = 24.8, so you have a BMI of 24.8.

The World Health Organisation use the following divisions to show where you are on the BMI range:
    Less than 18.5 – underweight
    18.5–24.9 – healthy weight
    25–29.9 – overweight
    30–34.9 – obese class I
    35–39.9 – obese class II*
    40 or more – obese class III

*If your BMI is more than 35, you need to see your doctor, as the extra weight may be putting your health at risk.

2) Find out how many calories you actually need:
First, calculate your basal metabolic rate (BMR) – that's the amount of calories your body needs to function).

BMR = weight (in kilos) x 2 x 11 (if you prefer to work in pounds that would be your weight in pounds x 11). For example, if you weight 65 kilos, your BMR = 65 x 2 x 11 = 1,430.

Now you need to work out how many extra calories you expend as a result of the activity you take. The best way to do this is to multiply your BMR by the following amounts according to which description of your exercise level is most appropriate to your lifestyle:
    If you are inactive or sedentary: BMR x 20 per cent
    If you are fairly active – for example, if you walk and take exercise once or twice a week: BMR x 30 per cent
    If you are moderately active, that is, you exercise two or three times a week: BMR x 40 per cent
    If you are active, that is, you exercise hard more than three times a week: BMR x 50 per cent
    If you are very active, that is, you exercise regularly each day: BMR x 70 per cent

Therefore, if you are a fairly active 65-kg woman – 1,430 x 30 per cent = 429.
Add this figure to your BMR to find out how many calories you need a day: 1,430 + 429 = 1,859.
Anything you eat on top of this will end up being stored as fat.

4 Do you take any exercise?

How much exercise do you do each day? A short walk once a week? A daily stroll to the bus stop?

England's Chief Medical Officer recommends that we do 30 minutes of exercise five times a week, but statistics show that eight out of ten women don't take anything like enough exercise.

A lack of exercise can cause and compound cellulite on several levels. Firstly, the more sedentary you are, the more likely you are to be overweight, which means more of those fat cells bulging out beneath your skin.

Secondly, when you exercise, you build muscle which helps boost the skin's collagen and elastin fibres, meaning that you effectively lift the skin, which can help prevent the puckering that takes place when the fibres pull downwards.

One study from the South Shore University in Massachusetts, in the USA, found that 70 per cent of women said their cellulite improved in just six weeks by doing aerobic exercise and weight training on their legs.

When you don't exercise, your lymphatic drainage system and your circulation pay the price of your inactivity. Think of your thighs and bottom containing healthy fatty tissue that has a blood supply which provides it with oxygen and nutrients and, as it drains away, removes waste products and fluid. When you are sedentary, your blood and lymph vessels become compressed. As a result, your body's cells are deprived of the oxygen and the blood circulation that effectively feeds your cells and keeps them healthy. And, in turn, the fibres around the fat cells become damaged and fluid builds up.

Studies have found that cellulite has more proteoglycans than 'normal' skin, which are cells that attract water. The lymphatic system, when it is working effectively, is responsible for pumping fluids round the body to the lymph glands where they are processed and from where they are eventually removed. If your lymphatic drainage system becomes sluggish – which happens when we're inactive – fluids build up, making cellulite look more bumpy.

The majority of us do tend to spend most of our lives sitting down – simply because we have sedentary jobs. But just by moving more you can dramatically improve the appearance of cellulite.

5 How good (or bad) is your diet?

Too many calories, for a start, cause your body to lay down extra stores of fat. Fatty, sugary foods provide lots of calories, but little in the way of body boosting nutrients, so if you have a sweet tooth, or can't say no to fatty foods, now's the time to take a look at your diet.

Not drinking enough water can also cause your lymphatic drainage system to slow down; basically if you're not drinking enough fluids your body will try to hold on to those it already has, which is why your cells stay stuffed with fluid. Water also helps keep your kidneys working optimally; drinking plenty of water helps them do their important job of diluting the body's waste products and helping eliminate them from the body.

The Natural Mineral Water Information Service estimates that about 90 per cent of us don't get enough fluids and this deficiency has been linked to all sorts of ailments, from headaches, lethargy and dry skin to digestive problems. The British Dietetic Association recommends that a 60-kg adult drinks 1.5–2 litres (6–8 250 ml glasses) of fluids a day – plenty of which should be water. Alternatively, aim for about 30 ml of water per kg of your body weight – or one litre for every 1,000 calories of food you consume.

Some experts also believe that certain food intolerances can compound the cellulite problem because they exacerbate fluid retention. Wheat and dairy intolerances are the most common. This is a debatable point, but the diet recommended in the 30-day programme has been designed to omit wheat and dairy products.

If you think you are intolerant to some foods, see your doctor. Perhaps you could try first to cut out meat or dairy from your diet for a week or so. Try keeping track of the results in a diary to see if you notice a difference. But make sure you are still eating a balanced diet. Instead of eating wheat, get your fibre from brown rice and fruits and veggies. Good sources of calcium are canned or oily fish and dried fruit. Soya milks, yoghurts and desserts are good alternatives to their dairy-based equivalents for lactose-intolerant people.

Salty foods are thought to be another cellulite trigger. Eating too much salt can be a factor in high blood pressure, and can cause stroke and heart disease. It can also increase your risk of stomach cancer, may aggravate asthma, and can cause osteoporosis. Plus too much salt can cause water retention. That's because your body holds on to fluid to help dilute the extra salt. Eating plenty of potassium-rich and low-sodium foods will help maintain a healthy salt balance in the body. The FSA (Food Standards Agency) recommends a daily intake of no more than 5 g salt (2 g sodium) each day. Keeping an eye on processed foods can also help. Avoid, or cut down, on big culprits, which include most stock cubes, salted and cured meats, packet soups and sauce mixes, processed cheese, hard cheese, salted butter and spreads.

Try retraining your taste buds: the sodium receptors on your tongue can be desensitised to salt in as little as two or three weeks. Instead of using salt to flavour your foods, try fresh herbs, spices, lemon juice or mustard. Use fresh ingredients to make your meal – apparently, 70 per cent of our salt intake comes from processed or pre-prepared foods. So get into the habit of reading labels when shopping for food. As a rule, foods that contain more than 0.5 g of sodium per serving are high in sodium. Foods than contain less than 0.1g of sodium are considered to be low-sodium foods.

6 Do you indulge in 'lifestyle nasties' – smoking, drinking, caffeine, sun worshipping?

Anything that can damage your skin can theoretically exacerbate cellulite. Smoking, alcohol and sunbathing can all cause the production of free radicals, which are molecules that lead to the breakdown of the cells that causes skin ageing or disease. They're known as 'unstable' molecules because they are missing a negative charge and, in order to find it from your body, they attack your body's other cells, which in turn produces more and more free radicals. This basically places the collagen in your skin at risk of attack, resulting in reduced elasticity, more wrinkles and sagging. All these factors can increase the appearance of cellulite. Which of these are you guilty of?

Too much caffeine: Large amounts of caffeine have been found to impede your blood flow – and healthy skin requires a regular blood circulation. Caffeine has a diuretic effect so it can also dehydrate your body.

Too much alcohol: A 'few drinks' can reduce your circulation, and cause dehydration, which robs the skin of moisture and vital nutrients. Some experts say spirits are far worse for your skin, because they cause an inflammatory reaction in it, which is potentially more damaging to your skin than the effects of wine.

Sunburn: Most of us feel our cellulite is less noticeable when we have a tan. But UVA rays also damage your skin by releasing harmful free radicals that alter the skin cells. That's when premature ageing takes place – enlarged pores, saggy skin and wrinkling. Avoid sunburn at all costs. Always use a sunscreen (experts recommend one with a minimum factor 15), and make sure you use enough. Reapply it often and stay out of the sun at the hottest part of the day. If you really want a tan, make it a fake one.

Smoking: Experts say that one single cigarette can reduce blood flow to the skin for more than an hour. When you smoke, blood vessels contract, which slows down the flow of oxygen to the skin. Every time you inhale, millions of free radicals enter the body, wreaking havoc with your skin – not just on your face – but all over your body.

Stress: Long-term stress raises your body's cortisol levels (cortisol is known as the 'death hormone' among dermatologists), depresses your body's natural growth hormone, DHEA, and undermines your immune system, all of which are important for healthy skin. Cortisol can also cause thinning of the skin, again making cellulite more noticeable. It may be easier said than done, but aim to relax – try meditation, regular massages, or even a walk in the park or countryside to help release tension.

7 It's your age?

Sadly, cellulite tends to get worse the older you get. There are a few reasons for this.

Age is another cause of collagen and elastin bundles breaking down and weakening the dermis. You know how this affects the skin on your face – you get wrinkles. And, as we have explained, this loss of dermal elasticity on your legs, bottom and stomach means the collagen fibres or 'connective tissue' around the fat parcels become less elastic. So they are less flexible, meaning that they don't 'give' when the fat squishes upwards, so the cellulite puckering is more obvious. Add to this the fact that your skin thins as you age, and you can see why cellulite looks worse the older you get.

Also, your muscle mass tends to decline by about 5 lb a decade after the age of 30. As a result your metabolic rate slows down, which means that if you carry on eating the same amount of food and calories, you'll gain weight; research shows that between the ages of 35 and 65 you gain about a pound a year. Combine that with the fact that we tend to become less active the older we get and it all means that we carry more fat, therefore the likelihood is that we will increase our cellulite. That's not to say that you're destined to live with the cellulite forever; the following programme can certainly help improve your cellulite in weeks. So, why not start today!

CHAPTER 3
THE INSPIRATION! – WHAT CAN HAPPEN AFTER 30 DAYS

Plan Results

The results you get from following the 30-Day Plan will obviously be personal to you, but we really wanted to see what happened for ourselves when the plan was put into action. We were lucky to find a group of lovely women who were all keen to see if they gained some benefit from the plan and on the following pages you will see some of the results.

A few women tested the diet by itself, while others tested the complete plan and used a home treatment (usually in the form of a cream). At the outset, we weighed and measured each tester. The measurements were taken from the following parts of the body: the waist, hips, widest part of the body (assessed individually), the thighs, the top of the left leg, middle of the left leg, just above the knee, top of the left arm, middle of the left arm and just above the elbow. The details provided with the 'before' and 'after' pictures in this section show the total inch loss for each tester.

Before you start the plan, you may also like to take your own measurements (or get someone to help you) and then take them again once you have completed the 30 days, so that you can see the difference.

In the meantime, we hope you find the following cases as inspirational as we do.

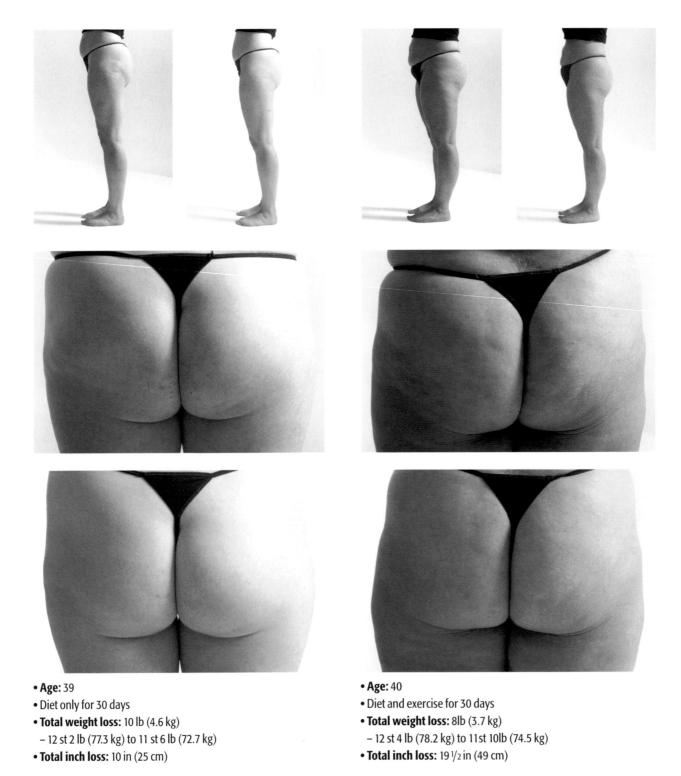

- **Age:** 39
- Diet only for 30 days
- **Total weight loss:** 10 lb (4.6 kg)
  – 12 st 2 lb (77.3 kg) to 11 st 6 lb (72.7 kg)
- **Total inch loss:** 10 in (25 cm)

- **Age:** 40
- Diet and exercise for 30 days
- **Total weight loss:** 8lb (3.7 kg)
  – 12 st 4 lb (78.2 kg) to 11st 10lb (74.5 kg)
- **Total inch loss:** 19 1/2 in (49 cm)

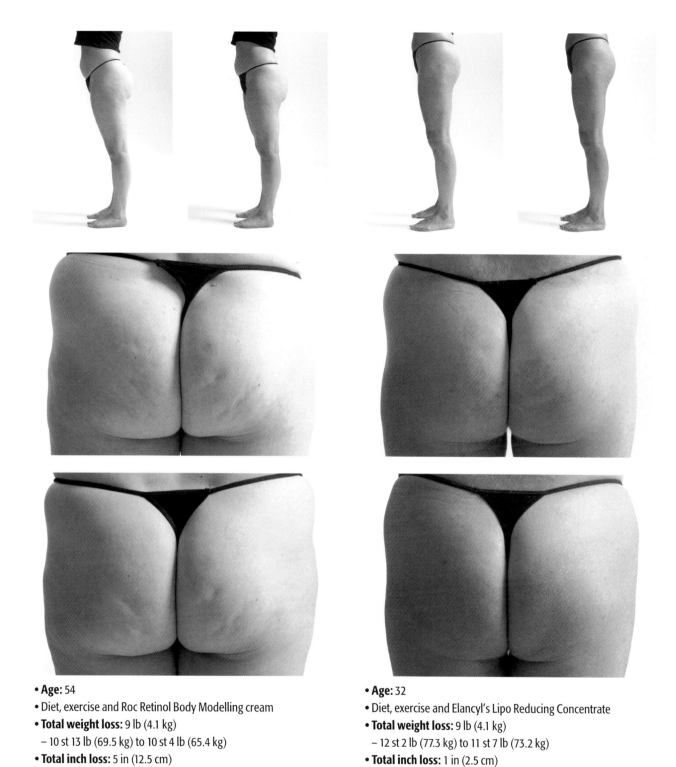

- **Age:** 54
- Diet, exercise and Roc Retinol Body Modelling cream
- **Total weight loss:** 9 lb (4.1 kg)
  – 10 st 13 lb (69.5 kg) to 10 st 4 lb (65.4 kg)
- **Total inch loss:** 5 in (12.5 cm)

- **Age:** 32
- Diet, exercise and Elancyl's Lipo Reducing Concentrate
- **Total weight loss:** 9 lb (4.1 kg)
  – 12 st 2 lb (77.3 kg) to 11 st 7 lb (73.2 kg)
- **Total inch loss:** 1 in (2.5 cm)

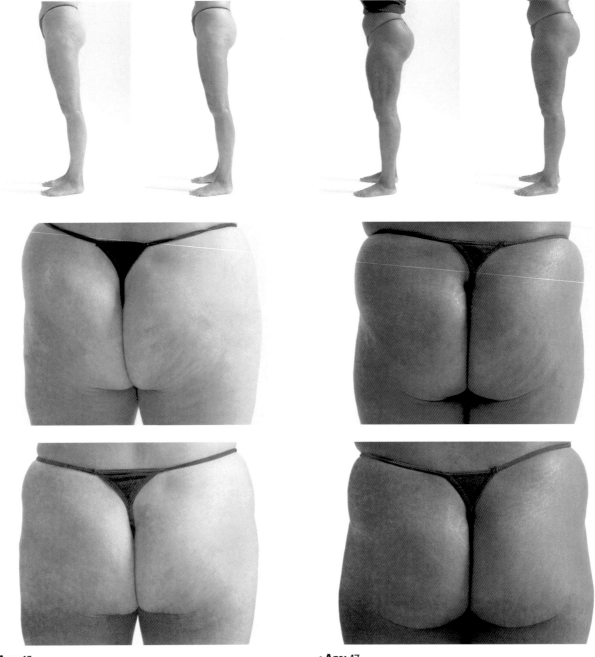

- **Age:** 43
- Diet, exercise and Dior's Bikini Celluli-Diet Body Defining Essence
- **Total weight loss:** 10 lb (4.6 kg)
  - 10 st 12 lb (69.1 kg) to 10 st 2 lb (64.4 kg)
- **Total inch loss:** 5 in (12.5 cm)

- **Age:** 47
- Diet, exercise and the Decléor Arromessence Contour series
- **Total weight loss:** 5 lb (2.3 kg)
  - 10 st 5 lb (65.9 kg) to 10 st (63.6 kg)
- **Total inch loss:** 4 in (10 cm)

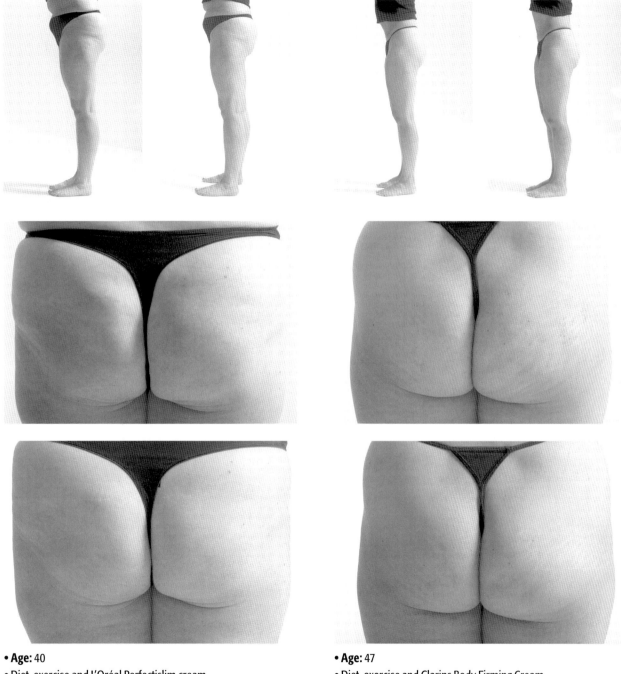

- **Age:** 40
- Diet, exercise and L'Oréal Perfectislim cream
- **Total weight loss:** 9 lb (4.1 kg)
  – 13 st 4 lb (84.5 kg) to 12 st 11 lb (80.4 kg)
- **Total inch loss:** 8 in (20 cm)

- **Age:** 47
- Diet, exercise and Clarins Body Firming Cream
- **Total weight loss:** 5lb (2.3 kg)
  – 9 st 6 lb (60 kg) to 9 st 1 lb (57.7 kg)
- **Total inch loss:** 6in (15 cm)

CHAPTER 4
THE 30-DAY PLAN

Now you know what you're dealing with and why you have cellulite, it's time to tackle it!

This 30-day programme combines a specially designed diet with an exercise programme and recommends skin brushing and the use of an anti-cellulite cream or other product designed to combat cellulite.

Yes, you will need some willpower, but after 30 days, you should see a firmer, fitter and less-cellulite-afflicted you.

Every day has a timetable for you to follow with boxes for you to tick once you have completed something. Obviously, we all lead busy lives and you may have to adjust the timetable to suit your lifestyle, but you should aim to fit everything in, even if you don't do it in the order suggested here. For example, you may prefer to do your 15 minutes of aerobic exercise in the evening before the exercises, or perhaps during your lunch break at work. Similarly, in the case of the diet, preparing the suggested lunch may not be possible because of the facilities available to you at work. If that is the case, try and compose your own packed lunch or salad by following the recommendations regarding food in the diet section that follows.

The details of the programme start on page 36, but the following pages contain information on the principles of the diet and the exercise programme. For more information about skin brushing and choosing a cream or anti-cellulite product, read the section on home treatments (page 66). Do read these first, so that you can adapt the programme to suit your personal needs.

We've added tick boxes to make it easier for you. So, once you've completed the task, tick the box and feel proud of yourself.

The diet

Although cellulite can affect any woman, no matter what her weight, the chances are that if you have cellulite you are probably also overweight. This diet aims primarily to help you lose the excess weight, and in doing so cleanse your system and flush out the toxins and get rid of the fat deposits which have caused the cellulite. And the most effective way to lose fat and keep it off is regular exercise plus a healthy and careful calorie intake. However, if you consider that you do not need to lose a lot of weight, then you may need to eat slightly larger portions than are recommended, or supplement this diet with extra nuts or snacks which follow the diet guidelines.

There are no magic foods that will melt cellulite away, but making just a few simple changes and learning to eat sensibly means you'll lose those extra pounds.

How fast can I lose weight?

Experts agree that between $\frac{1}{2}$ and 1 kilo (1–2 lb) per week is a healthy and effective rate of weight loss. A loss of more than 1 kilo (2 lb) per week means that you could be losing muscle.

The only way to lose fat is to take in fewer calories than your body needs for basic functions and daily activities: $\frac{1}{2}$ kilo (1 lb) of fat contains roughly 3,500 calories so, if you want to lose $\frac{1}{2}$ kg a week, then you have to lose 500 calories a day. The best way to cut 500 calories a day is to lose 250 calories through eating less and burn 250 calories through exercising. You can cut 250 calories by foregoing two biscuits and drinking one less glass of wine. Taking small, regular meals keeps your metabolism revved and is a much better way to burn off calories than, say, having one or two big meals a day. Your metabolism is boosted by about 10 per cent for 2–3 hours after you eat. Avoid skipping meals or leaving gaps longer than 5 hours between meals. Leaving long gaps between meals sends your body into starvation mode, triggering it to burn muscle instead of fat.

Researchers have found that people who eat breakfast are a third less likely to be obese compared with those who skip the meal. Eating first thing in the morning kick-starts your metabolism and allows you the whole day to burn up those calories. It also helps to stabilise blood sugar levels, which regulates your appetite and energy – so you're less likely to be hungry during the rest of the day and snack on unhealthy foods.

A combination of carbohydrate and protein (say, porridge, or yoghurt with fruit) will give you sustained energy.

COMMIT TO CHANGE

Write down three reasons why you want to get rid of your cellulite and lose weight. This will focus your mind on achieving your goal. If you have a good enough reason for doing something, you'll be motivated to stay the course. Keep this list where you can see it each day, such as on your fridge door or your desk. Reading the list every day will constantly remind you of what you want to achieve.

VISUALISE

Use your powers of visualisation and see yourself how you want to look. Imagine what you will be wearing, how you will be feeling and what your life will be like. Use an old photo of yourself that you like or a magazine photo for inspiration.

Dieting guidelines

EAT FIVE PORTIONS OF FRUIT AND VEGETABLES A DAY

Five daily portions of fruit and veg not only help protect against cancer and heart disease, but also fill you up and stop you snacking on high-calorie foods. Oranges, kiwi fruit, tomatoes, red peppers and strawberries are rich in vitamin C, which strengthens collagen and improves the appearance of cellulite.

WHAT'S A PORTION?

1 medium fruit: apples, oranges, bananas, peaches and pears
2 small fruit: satsumas, apricots, plums and kiwi fruit
1 cupful of berry-type fruit: grapes, strawberries, raspberries and cherries
$1/2$ **large fruit:** mangos, papayas and grapefruits
1 glass fruit juice: all 100 per cent fruit juices (not fruit drinks)
1 dessert bowlful of mixed salad vegetables: lettuces, salad leaves
2 tbsp cooked vegetables: broccoli, cauliflower, carrots and green beans
$1/2$ **cup of pulses:** baked beans, kidney beans, lentils and chickpeas

DON'T EAT A BIG MEAL IN THE EVENING

Eating a lot of calories in the evening when you are inactive increases the chances of storing them as body fat. Try to eat a smaller meal, comprised mainly of vegetables and lean protein. Avoid eating during the two hours before retiring to bed.

REPLACE HALF YOUR CARBOHYDRATES WITH VEGGIES

Cut back on starchy foods – potatoes, bread and pasta – and fill up instead with plenty of vegetables, salad and fresh fruit. Try replacing half your usual portion of pasta (or whatever) with vegetables, such as carrots, broccoli, green beans or cauliflower. That way you won't feel as though you are eating less.

LIMIT YOUR FOOD CHOICES

Research at Tufts University in Massachusetts shows that, when people are presented with a wider variety of foods, they eat considerably more. The message here is to simplify your diet. Next time you are faced with a glorious choice, opt for only two or three types of food rather than a bit of everything.

DON'T BE FAT PHOBIC

Don't try to cut fat out completely as this would be unhealthy and hinder your progress. Including foods rich in essential fats – oily fish, avocados, nuts, olives and seeds – in moderation can help you burn body fat more efficiently and boost your immunity.

REMEMBER DRINKS COUNT TOO

Alcohol calories count too and, if you knock back a few drinks in an evening, they can sabotage your fat-loss plan. One glass of wine contains 85–125 calories and a bottle of lager contains 130 calories. If you must drink, limit yourself to one small glass of wine a day.

PACK A (HEALTHY) SNACK

Always carry healthy snacks, such as apples, satsumas or nuts, with you so that you don't feel the urge to grab a bar of chocolate or biscuit when you're out and about.

EAT SOUP

Have a bowl of soup for starters and you'll find that it curbs your appetite. Research at the University of Pennsylvania found that, if you have soup as a first course, you end up eating fewer calories. Avoid creamy soups, though; stick to vegetable varieties (see recipes on pages 81 – 82).

GIVE UP READY MEALS

Give up ready meals and takeaways as they're packed full of salt, calories and fat. Instead cook for yourself – try the recipes in the 30-Day Plan and you'll be eating so much more healthily.

HAVE FRUIT FOR STARTERS

Eat a piece of fruit before your meal. According to a Brazilian study, women who ate an apple or pear before a meal lost more weight than those who didn't. Fruit is a good source of fibre, too, and a high-fibre diet can help you lose weight because you feel fuller for longer.

SNACK ON NUTS

Snacking on nuts will improve your heart health without making you gain weight. In a US study, people who added 500 calories' worth of peanuts lowered the level of fats in their blood without changing their body weight. Researchers suggest that the nuts made them feel full so that they ate fewer calories overall, or the nuts boosted their metabolic rate so that they burned more calories.

THIRSTY OR HUNGRY?

Many people confuse thirst with hunger. Next time you're feeling peckish, drink a glass of water and wait 10 minutes to see if you are still hungry. Water is an essential nutrient that helps your body burn fat.

EAT FRUIT INSTEAD OF DRINKING JUICE

Fruit juice and dried fruit contain much higher concentrations of (natural) sugar than the fresh fruit they came from. Swapping a glass of orange juice for an orange saves 60 calories; and eating a small bunch of grapes instead of a small handful of raisins saves 100 calories.

GO FOR A WALK AFTER A MEAL

Gentle exercise, such as walking, after eating may turn more of the calories that you have just eaten into heat and make your body burn more calories. Similarly, eating in the hour after vigorous exercise encourages it to be turned into energy rather than stored as fat, as the metabolic rate is speeded up during this time.

The food solution

LIGHTEN YOUR LIVER LOAD

Include foods that stimulate the detoxifying process. Cruciferous vegetables (Brussels sprouts, broccoli, cabbage and cauliflower) contain glucosinolates, which help liver enzymes work efficiently. Onions and garlic contain sulphur compounds, which aid detoxification; while watercress, tomatoes, carrots and apples are rich in nutrients (such as vitamin C and vitamin E), which help the liver do its job properly.

STRENGTHEN YOUR SKIN FROM WITHIN

To make skin look smoother, you should include foods that help nourish the skin and strengthen the collagen, the building blocks supporting the fat cells that stop skin sagging. Omega-3 fatty acids are very good for the texture of the skin and improve its elasticity – you will find them in flax seed oil, walnuts and walnut oil, oily fish and omega-3-rich oil blends.

Brightly coloured fruits and vegetables, nuts (almonds, cashews, walnuts and brazils), seeds (flax, pumpkin, sesame and sunflower), and olives also promote firm, smooth skin.

BOOST YOUR CIRCULATION

Fat cells in cellulite-affected areas often have a poor blood supply as blood and lymph vessels become compressed. Regular exercise and shedding surplus weight helps restore blood circulation, but eating foods with a blood-thinning effect may also help. These include onions, garlic, nuts and foods rich in omega-3 fatty acids, such as flax oil, walnut oil, pumpkin seeds, oily fish and omega-3-rich oil blends.

BEAT FLUID RETENTION

Eating foods rich in potassium and low in sodium (salt), such as fresh fruit, vegetables and whole grains, will help rebalance minerals salts in your body and so eliminate excess fluid that makes the fat pockets under your skin become dimply. Ironically, drinking more water also helps eliminate fluid retention and the cellulite that this can trigger. You need to drink plenty of water to

flush out the excess sodium. As we've put in the programme, you should aim for 6–8 glasses a day. Count fruit juices (ideally, diluted with water), herb and fruit teas towards your daily target.

REDUCE FREE RADICAL DAMAGE

Eat plenty of foods rich in antioxidant nutrients – brightly coloured fruit, dark green leafy vegetables, nuts and seeds – to combat free-radical damage caused by pollution, UV light, smoking, alcohol, caffeine and saturated fats. Excess free radicals wreak havoc in your body weaken the skin's collagen and elastin.

Eat these

FRESH FRUIT AND VEGETABLES

As well as fibre, fresh fruit and vegetables are rich in vitamins (especially vitamins A and C), minerals, antioxidants and other important plant nutrients, which help promote good circulation, cell renewal and liver function. The antioxidants contained in brightly coloured fruits such as oranges, blueberries, strawberries and raspberries help destroy free radicals and are vital for your lymphatic system.

HEALTHY FATS AND OILS

Food rich in essential fatty acids – olive oil, flaxseed oil, walnut oil, nuts, seeds and oily fish – are good for the skin and strengthening connective tissue around the fat cells. Other good sources include nuts (such as walnuts, cashews and almonds) and seeds (pumpkin, flax, sesame and sunflower).

BEANS, LENTILS AND WHOLE GRAINS

Beans, lentils and whole grains break down more slowly during digestion and have a low glycaemic index (see the box *The glycaemic index explained* opposite), producing a sustained rise in blood sugar. They don't trigger the surges of insulin associated with high GI foods (sugary foods and refined carbohydrates) and therefore are less likely to be stored as fat.

There is a theory that pesticide residues found in non-organic food disrupt your metabolism, interfere with your body's ability to convert food into energy and make you gain weight. As organic food is free from pesticide residues, it may help you on the road to weight loss. Eating less non-organic food allows the liver and the rest of the body to work properly and means that calories are burnt off more efficiently. There is also evidence that organic fruit and vegetables contain more vitamin C, magnesium and iron than conventional varieties but, if you can't go organic, wash, clean and peel fruit and vegetables before eating them. Cooking vegetables, rather than eating them raw, also washes off and destroys chemicals.

THE GLYCAEMIC INDEX EXPLAINED

The Glycaemic Index (GI) ranks all carbohydrate foods according to the effect that they have on your blood sugar level, against a glucose standard, which rates 100, the fastest of all carbohydrates to be absorbed into your bloodstream.

Avoid these

CAFFEINE

Unfortunately, caffeine found in coffee, tea, colas and 'energy drinks', hardens the walls of blood vessels and restricts blood supply – something that your cellulite-affected areas desperately need. Drinking more than three cups of coffee a day can leave you feeling tired, irritable and fatigued. If you normally drink caffeine drinks, cut back gradually over a week or two to avoid withdrawal symptoms (notably headaches). Smart alternatives include herbal tea (such as peppermint, camomile and fennel), fruit tea, green tea (although not caffeine free, caffeine levels are lower than coffee and regular tea) and hot water with lemon.

ALCOHOL

A moderate amount of alcohol – around one drink a day – dilates blood vessels and boosts blood flow. Studies have also shown that it helps protect against heart disease, increase longevity and even prevent the onset of diabetes. However, higher amounts can push up blood fat levels, restrict blood flow and impair liver function. Alcohol can also dehydrate your body, exacerbating cellulite, and increase the number of free radicals in your body. During the 30-Day Plan, if you can't live without it, limit yourself to one small glass of wine a day.

SUGAR

Sugar provides empty calories. It has no vitamins and minerals that you need to release energy from food. Sugary foods also tend to be high in fat and calories; they have very little 'filling' power, so are easy to over-consume and convert into unwanted fat. Some experts believe that a high intake of sugar causes collagen to harden, making the fibres around your fat cells distorted and creating dimples.

Try to cut out added sugars completely, instead opt for foods containing natural sugars – fresh and dried fruit, vegetables and fruit-based smoothies. In their natural state, sugars come with a package of water, fibre and vitamins.

SATURATED AND PROCESSED (TRANS) FATS

Minimising saturated and trans fats is crucial. These fats raise levels of bad low-density lipoprotein (LDL) blood cholesterol and cause a fatty cholesterol-rich build-up on blood vessel walls, which restricts blood flow to your cells. So cut out butter, meat, eggs, full-fat dairy products, fast food, processed foods (such as cakes, pastries, biscuits and pies) and anything that lists hydrogenated fats or partially hydrogenated fats on the label. The latter two ingredients contain high levels of trans fats, formed when hydrogen gas is added to vegetable oils to make them more solid. Studies have shown that trans fats raise levels of bad LDL cholesterol in your body to a greater extent than saturated fats, while also reducing levels of good HDL cholesterol, something saturated fat doesn't do. There's no safe minimum amount of trans fat – they are best avoided altogether.

REFINED CARBOHYDRATES

Avoid white bread, ordinary pasta and anything made with white flour during the 30-Day Plan as they can produce rapid surges of sugar in the bloodstream, triggering the release of excessive insulin, and fat storage. Over time, the body becomes less sensitive to insulin, which means it produces more, increasing the amount of fat stored. Also a diet high in refined carbohydrates causes an increase in blood fat levels and a drop in HDL (good) cholesterol.

SALT

A high salt intake causes fluid retention and bloating, as well as putting a strain on your circulatory and lymphatic systems. Over time, having too much salt (sodium) can result in high blood pressure, which increases the risk of heart disease and stroke. The UK Food Standards Agency (FSA) recommends eating no more than 6 g daily (the current average is 9–10 g). Lots of processed foods are high in salt, including breakfast cereals, soups, ready meals and sauces. Cut down on these and try to make your own meals from scratch – see the recipes in the 30-Day Plan. The FSA defines anything containing more than 1.25 g salt per 100 g as high. Choose foods containing less than this amount.

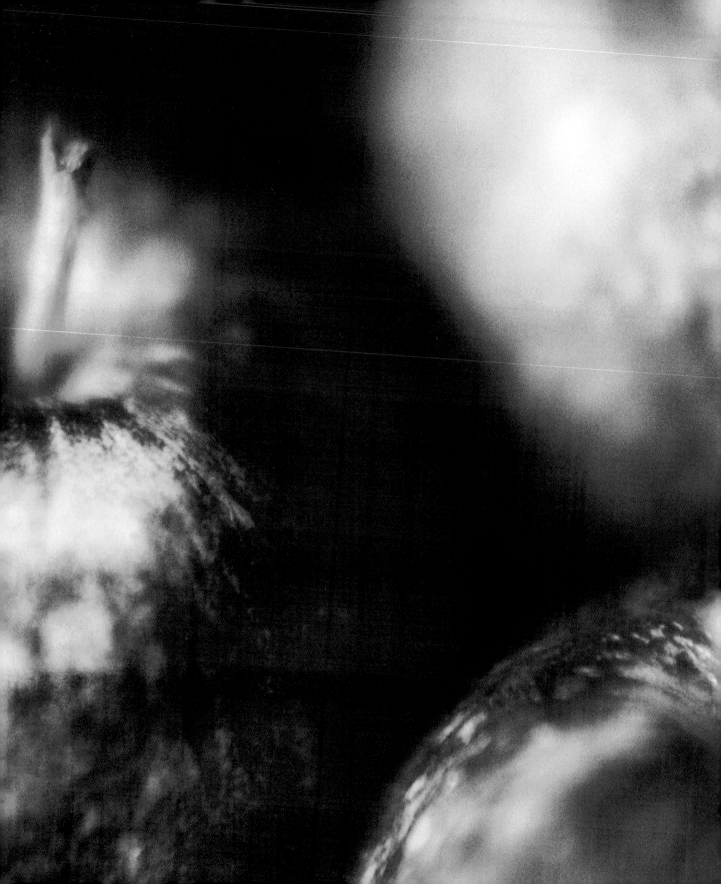

Try flavouring food with herbs, freshly ground black pepper, lemon or lime juice, spices or use a low-sodium salt (which is based on potassium and contains around two-thirds less sodium than ordinary salt) in cooking.

WHEAT
Wheat-based foods – in bread, cakes, pastries, pasta, biscuits and breakfast cereals – can encourage water retention – which can exacerbate the appearance of cellulite. Some experts also believe that over-exposure to wheat over a period of time leads to food intolerances. These may give rise to symptoms such as bloating, headaches and lethargy after eating them. During the 30-day plan, try cutting out wheat and replacing it with other cereals, such as rice, oats (although not gluten-free, they are usually tolerated well) and corn.

ANIMAL PROTEIN
Proteins found in meat, poultry, fish, eggs and dairy produce are acid forming – they leave acid residues after digestion, raising the acidity level in the blood. This is considered to be destructive to body tissues and, in the short term, an acid-forming diet stresses the body's detoxification capacity. Organs can function properly only in a slightly alkaline environment, so any acid residues have to be alkalised by the body's buffering systems. These use up certain minerals such as calcium and potassium. In the long term, an acid-producing diet can leach calcium from the bones, causing them to become weaker and thinner.

As well as cutting down on acid-producing foods, you should boost your intake of alkaline-producing foods: all fruits, vegetables, nuts and seeds.

However, it is not necessary to cut out all acid-producing foods, otherwise you might miss out on protein and other important minerals. For this reason, fish (including oily fish) can be included from time to time (for its omega-3 oil content) as well as grains, beans, lentils and yoghurt (for its calcium).

Cellulite super-foods

APPLES AND PEARS
Both of these fruits have a gentle laxative and diuretic effect, helping rid the body of unwanted toxins and reduce water retention. They contain pectin, a soluble fibre that stimulates the natural muscular contractions of the bowel and keeps the colon healthy. Pectin also helps to lower blood cholesterol levels. Apples and pears are excellent sources of potassium, which helps rebalance fluid levels in the body, prevent water retention and improve the appearance of cellulite. They also provide many vitamins and minerals, including vitamin C, as well as natural cancer-fighting compounds. Eat unpeeled to maximise their fibre content and also because the nutrients are concentrated near and within the skin.

AVOCADO
Avocados are packed with many nutrients that can slow the ageing process and improve the health of the skin. They are rich in monounsaturates – fats that help the skin combat free radicals – and vitamin E, which promotes healthy skin and slows the ageing process. Add avocados to salads or fill half an avocado with chopped tomatoes and pumpkin seeds.

BERRIES
Berries – blueberries, blackcurrants, strawberries and raspberries – are one of the best foods for your skin. They are packed with polyphenols, antioxidants that help fight the damaging effects of free radicals. Blueberries are particularly rich in anthocyanins, the antioxidant purple pigment that helps strengthen capillary walls and maintain blood flow through tiny vessels deep inside connective tissues.

BROCCOLI
Broccoli and other cruciferous vegetables (Brussels sprouts, cauliflower, cabbage) are packed with antioxidants and fibre.

They not only benefit the digestive system but also stimulate the liver. When the liver works to its full potential, so do all the other systems in the body. When the toxic load in the body is reduced, the skin visibly improves – and that includes cellulite-affected areas. Broccoli is also rich in vitamin C, folic acid, calcium and beta-carotene. Steam lightly to conserve the nutrients.

CARROTS

Carrots are extremely detoxifying, strengthening the liver function. They are one of the richest sources of beta-carotene, a powerful antioxidant, which helps keep the skin soft and smooth and prevents dryness and wrinkling. The beta-carotene is best absorbed when eaten with a little oil (such as in stir-fries) or eaten as part of a dressed salad, or juiced.

HUMMUS

Chickpeas, the key ingredient in hummus, contain fructo-oligosaccharides, a type of fibre that maintains a healthy balance of bacteria (flora) in your gut. Like all types of beans and lentils, chickpeas are a good source of protein and slow-release carbohydrates. These do not send a sudden surge of sugar in the blood, causing peaks and troughs in energy levels. They give a sustained source of energy, helping to stabilise blood sugar levels and control your appetite. Hummus also supplies calcium, important for breaking down body fat, and iron, which is needed for making healthy red blood cells.

KIWI FRUIT

One large kiwi fruit provides all of your daily vitamin C needs – more than an equivalent sized orange – crucial for the building of collagen, the building blocks that support your skin. Vitamin C also helps strengthen the capillaries (tiny blood vessels) and cell walls. Kiwi fruit are also packed with beta-carotene, which combats cell-damaging free radicals, and flavanoids, which, along with vitamin C, also help strengthen blood capillaries. They are good sources of blood-pressure-regulating potassium, as well as folate, an essential vitamin that helps protect against heart disease.

NUTS

A good source of protein, nuts are also full of nutrients, including vitamin E, zinc, magnesium, iron and B vitamins. Vitamin E helps improve your circulation as well as your skin. Although nuts are high in fat, this is mainly monounsaturated fat, which helps lower blood cholesterol levels. Brazil nuts are a good source of selenium, a potent antioxidant that helps reduce signs of ageing. One brazil provides most of your daily needs for this mineral. Walnuts contain omega-3 oils, which not only lower blood cholesterol but also improve the appearance of the skin.

OATS

Oats consumed daily can help lower cholesterol, thus preventing blood vessels furring up. They contain beta-glucan, a soluble fibre that mops up the precursors of cholesterol and whisks them out of the body. Another plus is that the fibre in oats makes you feel full fast. That should prevent you overeating, keep hunger pangs at bay and help you lose weight. Oats are also one of few grains to contain vitamin E – a powerful antioxidant that protects your skin from ageing.

PUMPKIN SEEDS

Pumpkin seeds (and also flax seeds) are packed with omega-3 oils, which not only lower your heart disease risk but also benefit your skin, reducing the appearance of cellulite. They are a good source of vitamin E, which works with other antioxidants, to keep the skin healthy by protecting it from antioxidants. Sprinkle on muesli, salads, yoghurt or nibble instead of crisps and other snacks.

SPINACH

Green leafy vegetables such as spinach are rich in vitamin K, which thins the blood slightly making it flow more freely and so improves the supply of oxygen and nutrients to cellulite-affected areas. They are also full of lutein, an antioxidant that helps prevent wrinkles and combat ageing. Spinach contains iron, a mineral needed for making red blood cells, which transport oxygen around the body. Serve spinach lightly steamed or raw in salads to maximise the vitamin content.

The exercise programme

Within the 30-Day Plan, there are instructions as to when to exercise. As we mentioned at the start of this section, there is some flexibility as to when you complete the exercise routines or aerobic exercise, but you must try and fit it all in.

This anti-cellulite plan consists of repetitions of exercises targeting the muscle groups of the thighs, buttocks and other lumpy cellulite-prone areas.

You will find the details of the exercises and full instructions on how to complete each one in chapter 8 on page 108. It is extremely important to stretch out the muscles after each exercise: doing so helps to increase the length and flexibility of the muscles, leading to improved strength and resulting in more muscle and less cellulite.

In addition to the exercises and stretches outlined in the programme, you should do fifteen minutes of aerobic exercise five times a week, for example, fast walking or jogging, swimming or any other aerobic exercise – the choice is yours. Or why not make this the moment you take up dancing classes or a martial art? If you do choose to walk, jog or swim, then save money by using outdoor facilities where possible: swimming pools (depending on the season, obviously), parks, roads, fields – anywhere freely accessible to the public. Always do a 2–4-minute warm up before and a 2–4-minute cool down after your session of aerobic exercise.

The exercise programme is not a miracle cure, but with time and dedication it will result in less cellulite.

When exercising and stretching, be aware of your body's limits and do not over-stretch – particularly if you do not exercise regularly. Be especially careful if you have any back or neck problems. Consult your doctor if you are unsure about doing any of the exercises in this programme.

The exercises and their complementary stretches

The programme is split into three sections: lower body, middle body and upper body. The exercises and complementary stretches for each section of the body should be completed twice a week and, by Day 22, up to four times a week.

If you want to focus on reducing cellulite on your buttocks, legs and inner and outer thighs, do the lunges and squats described below. Adding ankle weights or holding light weights at your sides will increase the intensity of the exercise and have more impact.

WARM UP
Skip or run lightly on the spot for 2–3 minutes to raise your heart rate slightly and get the blood flowing into your muscles . An effective alternative is 'spotty dogs' (see page 111).

COOL DOWN
When you have finished your aerobic exercise, or exercise session, cool down with a few of the stretches and make sure you keep yourself warm. This may sound strange if you've worked up a bit of a sweat as a result of the activity and are feeling hot, but your body can cool down quite rapidly and if it gets cold too quickly, your muscles can seize up and you may possibly suffer from cramp.

DAY 1

Early morning

❑ **On waking** – a glass of hot water with a slice of lemon (or you could have a cup of herbal tea as an alternative)

❑ **Exercise** – 15 minutes of aerobic exercise (this could be done during your lunch hour, if preferred)

❑ **Before showering** – brush skin, particularly the areas affected by cellulite (see page 67 for advice)

❑ Shower or bath

❑ Apply cream etc. (see page 70 for advice)

Morning

❑ **Breakfast** – Porridge with raisins and apricots (recipe page 84)

❑ Water

❑ **Mid-morning snack** – 2 rice crackers (rice cakes) topped with 2 tsp (10 ml) peanut butter

❑ Water

Afternoon

❑ **Lunch** – Carrot soup with fresh coriander (recipe page 81)
Slice of rye (or other non-wheat) bread or 2 rye or rice crackers
125 g (4 oz) fresh fruit (e.g. plums, peach or nectarine)

❑ Water

❑ **Mid-afternoon snack** – 125 g (4 oz) fresh fruit (e.g. strawberries, raspberries or blueberries)

❑ Water

Evening

❑ **Exercise** – Lower body exercises plus complementary stretches. Repeat each exercise continuously for 20 seconds. After each exercise, the complementary stretch should be held for 30 seconds.

❑ **Dinner** – Grilled aubergines with mint and yoghurt dressing (recipe page 86)
175 g (6 oz) steamed green vegetables (e.g. broccoli or Brussels sprouts)

❑ Water

❑ **Before bed** – apply cream as directed, if necessary

DAY 2

Early morning

❏ **On waking** – a glass of hot water with a slice of lemon

❏ **Exercise** – 15 minutes of aerobic exercise

❏ **Before showering** – brush skin, particularly the areas affected by cellulite

❏ Shower or bath

❏ Apply cream etc.

Morning

❏ **Breakfast** – 1 pot of plain soya yoghurt or natural bio-yoghurt mixed with 1 tsp (5 ml) clear honey and 125 g (4 oz) fresh fruit (e.g. banana, nectarine or apple)

❏ Water

❏ **Mid-morning snack** – 4 brazil nuts

❏ Water

Afternoon

❏ **Lunch** – Romaine salad with honey and mustard dressing (recipe page 95)
1 small jacket potato with a little olive oil spread
125 g (4 oz) fresh fruit (e.g. strawberries or raspberries)

❏ Water

❏ **Mid-afternoon snack** – 1 banana

❏ Water

Evening

❏ **Exercise** – Upper body, middle body plus complementary stretches. Repeat each exercise continuously for 20 seconds. Use 2 kg hand weights or dumbbells for upper body exercises. After each exercise, the complementary stretch should be held for 30 seconds.

❏ **Dinner** – Stir-fried vegetables with cashews (recipe page 86)
125 g (4 oz) grilled tuna steak *or* 125 g (4 oz) stir-fried tofu
2 heaped tbsp (30 ml) cooked brown rice

❏ Water

❏ **Before bed** – apply cream as directed, if necessary

DAY 3

Early morning

- [ ] **On waking** – a glass of hot water with a slice of lemon

- [ ] **Exercise** – 15 minutes of aerobic exercise

- [ ] **Before showering** – brush skin, particularly the areas affected by cellulite

- [ ] Shower or bath

- [ ] Apply cream etc.

Morning

- [ ] **Breakfast** – Muesli with fruit and nuts (recipe page 84)

- [ ] Water

- [ ] **Mid-morning snack** – 1 pot plain soya yoghurt or natural bio-yoghurt mixed with 125 g (4 oz) chopped fresh fruit (e.g. strawberries, banana or blueberries)

- [ ] Water

Afternoon

- [ ] **Lunch** – Hummus (ready-made or recipe on page 94) Crudités (see page 93) Slice of rye (or other non-wheat) bread or 3 rye crackers with a little olive oil spread and honey 125 g (4 oz) fresh fruit (e.g. apple, grapes, satsumas, grapefruit)

- [ ] Water

- [ ] **Mid-afternoon snack** – A glass of fresh fruit juice

- [ ] Water

Evening

- [ ] **Exercise** – Lower body, middle body plus complementary stretches. Repeat each exercise continuously for 20 seconds. Use 2 kg hand weights or dumbbells for upper body exercises. After each exercise, the complementary stretch should be held for 30 seconds.

- [ ] **Dinner** – 1 small baked potato with a drizzle of olive oil Spinach with pine nuts (recipe page 89) Salad leaves with a little balsamic dressing

- [ ] Water

- [ ] **Before bed** – apply cream as directed, if necessary

DAY 4

Early morning

- ❏ **On waking** – a glass of hot water with a slice of lemon

- ❏ **Exercise** – 15 minutes of aerobic exercise

- ❏ **Before showering** – brush skin, particularly the areas affected by cellulite

- ❏ Shower or bath

- ❏ Apply cream etc.

Morning

- ❏ **Breakfast** – Porridge with raisins and apricots (recipe page 84)

- ❏ Water

- ❏ **Mid-morning snack** – 125 g (4 oz) fresh fruit (e.g. apple, pear or banana)

- ❏ Water

Afternoon

- ❏ **Lunch** – 1 small baked potato with a drizzle of extra virgin olive oil or flax seed oil
  1–2 tbsp (15–30 ml) hummus or guacamole (ready-bought or see recipes page 94)
  Mixed salad leaves
  125 g (4 oz) fresh fruit (e.g. peach, orange or kiwi fruit)

- ❏ Water

- ❏ **Mid-afternoon snack** – Smoothie (recipes pages 105–107)

- ❏ Water

Evening

- ❏ **Exercise** – Upper body exercises plus complementary stretches. Repeat each exercise continuously for 20 seconds. Use 2 kg hand weights or dumbbells for upper body exercises. After each exercise, the complementary stretch should be held for 30 seconds.

- ❏ **Dinner** – Rice noodles with vegetables in spiced coconut milk (recipe page 98)
  1 pot (150 ml) plain soya yoghurt or natural bio-yoghurt mixed with 1 tbsp (15 ml) muesli

- ❏ Water

- ❏ **Before bed** – apply cream as directed, if necessary

DAY 5

Early morning

- ❏ **On waking** – a glass of hot water with a slice of lemon

- ❏ **Exercise** – 15 minutes of aerobic exercise

- ❏ **Before showering** – brush skin, particularly the areas affected by cellulite

- ❏ Shower or bath

- ❏ Apply cream etc.

Morning

- ❏ **Breakfast** – Fruit and yoghurt (recipe page 85)

- ❏ Water

- ❏ **Mid-morning snack** – 125 g (4 oz) fresh fruit (e.g. plums, peach or nectarine)

- ❏ Water

Afternoon

- ❏ **Lunch** – Tomato and vegetable soup (recipe page 80)
  Slice of rye (or other non-wheat) bread or 2 rye or rice crackers
  125 g (4 oz) fresh fruit (e.g. strawberries, raspberries or blueberries)

- ❏ Water

- ❏ **Mid-afternoon snack** – 1 pot plain soya yoghurt or natural bio-yoghurt mixed with 3 chopped dried apricots

- ❏ Water

Evening

- ❏ **Exercise** – Lower body, middle body exercises plus complementary stretches. Repeat each exercise continuously for 20 seconds. Use 2 kg hand weights or dumbbells for upper body exercises. After each exercise, the complementary stretch should be held for 30 seconds.

- ❏ **Dinner** – Roasted Mediterranean vegetables with olive and rosemary (recipe page 90)
  2 heaped tbsp (30 ml) cooked brown rice
  85 g (3 oz) grilled white fish *or* 3 tbsp (45 ml) tinned beans (e.g. pinto beans, chickpeas)

- ❏ Water

- ❏ **Before bed** – apply cream as directed, if necessary

DAY 6

Early morning

- ❏ **On waking** – a glass of hot water with a slice of lemon

- ❏ **Before showering** – brush skin, particularly the areas affected by cellulite

- ❏ Shower or bath

- ❏ Apply cream etc.

Morning

- ❏ **Breakfast** – Compote of dried fruit (recipe page 85)

- ❏ Water

- ❏ **Mid-morning snack** – Small handful of toasted seeds (e.g. pumpkin, sunflower or sesame seeds)

- ❏ Water

Afternoon

- ❏ **Lunch** – Spinach, rocket and avocado salad (recipe page 95) Small handful of nuts (e.g. cashews, walnuts, peanuts) 1 pot (150 g) plain soya or natural bio-yoghurt mixed with 1 tbsp (15 ml) muesli

- ❏ Water

- ❏ **Mid-afternoon snack** – 125 g (4 oz) fresh fruit (e.g. oranges, satsumas, kiwi fruit)

- ❏ Water

Evening

- ❏ **Dinner** – 125 g (4 oz) grilled chicken breast, brushed with olive oil *or* lentil dahl with fresh coriander (recipe page 93) 2 heaped tbsp (30 ml) non-wheat pasta 225 g (8 oz) steamed vegetables (e.g. carrots, broccoli, courgettes, green beans)

- ❏ Water

- ❏ **Before bed** – apply cream as directed, if necessary

DAY 7

Early morning

- ❑ **On waking** – a glass of hot water with a slice of lemon

- ❑ **Before showering** – brush skin, particularly the areas affected by cellulite

- ❑ Shower or bath

- ❑ Apply cream etc.

Morning

- ❑ **Breakfast** – 225 g (8 oz) mixture of fresh fruit (e.g. melon, grapefruit, oranges, peaches, strawberries, kiwi fruit) 1–2 tbsp (15–30 ml) nuts (e.g. toasted almonds, hazelnuts or cashews

- ❑ Water

- ❑ **Mid-morning snack** – 125 g (4 oz) fresh fruit (e.g. peach, orange or kiwi fruit)

- ❑ Water

Afternoon

- ❑ **Lunch** – Cabbage, leek and broccoli soup with toasted almonds (recipe page 82) Slice of rye (or other non-wheat) bread or 2 rye or rice crackers 125 g (4 oz) fresh fruit (e.g. apple, pear or banana)

- ❑ Water

- ❑ **Mid-afternoon snack** – Carrot, celery and cucumber sticks dipped in a little hummus

- ❑ Water

Evening

- ❑ **Dinner** – Pasta with spring vegetables (recipe page 97) 1 pot plain soya yoghurt or natural bio-yoghurt mixed with 2 tbsp berries (e.g. strawberries, raspberries or blueberries)

- ❑ Water

- ❑ **Before bed** – apply cream as directed, if necessary

DAY 8

Early morning

- ❑ **On waking** – a glass of hot water with a slice of lemon

- ❑ **Exercise** – 15 minutes of aerobic exercise

- ❑ **Before showering** – brush skin, particularly the areas affected by cellulite

- ❑ Shower or bath

- ❑ Apply cream etc.

Morning

- ❑ **Breakfast** – Muesli with fruit and nuts (recipe page 84)

- ❑ Water

- ❑ **Mid-morning snack** – 2 rice crackers (rice cakes) topped with 2 tsp (10 ml) peanut butter

- ❑ Water

Afternoon

- ❑ **Lunch** – Carrot soup with fresh coriander (recipe page 81)
  Slice of rye (or other non-wheat) bread or 2 rye or rice crackers
  125 g (4 oz) fresh fruit (e.g. strawberries, raspberries or blueberries)

- ❑ Water

- ❑ **Mid-afternoon snack** – A glass of fresh fruit juice

- ❑ Water

Evening

- ❑ **Exercise** – Lower body plus complementary stretches. Repeat each exercise continuously for 30 seconds. After each exercise, the complementary stretch should be held for 30 seconds.

- ❑ **Dinner** – Quinoa and rice with pumpkin seeds (recipe page 89)
  Fresh fruit with honey (recipe page 102)

- ❑ Water

- ❑ **Before bed** – apply cream as directed, if necessary

DAY 9

Early morning

- ❏ **On waking** – a glass of hot water with a slice of lemon

- ❏ **Exercise** – 15 minutes of aerobic exercise

- ❏ **Before showering** – brush skin, particularly the areas affected by cellulite

- ❏ Shower or bath

- ❏ Apply cream etc.

Morning

- ❏ **Breakfast** – Porridge with raisins and apricots (recipe page 84)

- ❏ Water

- ❏ **Mid-morning snack** – 125 g (4 oz) fresh fruit (e.g. apple, pear or banana)

- ❏ Water

Afternoon

- ❏ **Lunch** – Guacamole (ready-made or recipe on page 94) Crudités (see page 93) Slice of rye (or other non-wheat) bread or 3 rye crackers with a little olive oil spread and honey 125 g (4 oz) fresh fruit (e.g. apple, grapes or pear)

- ❏ Water

- ❏ **Mid-afternoon snack** – 1 pot plain soya yoghurt or natural bio-yoghurt mixed with 1 tbsp (15 ml) muesli

- ❏ Water

Evening

- ❏ **Exercise** – Upper body, middle body exercises plus complementary stretches. Repeat each exercise continuously for 30 seconds Use 2 kg hand weights or dumbbells for upper body exercises. After each exercise, the complementary stretch should be held for 30 seconds.

- ❏ **Dinner** – Roasted root vegetables (recipe page 90) 100 g (3½ oz) grilled trout fillet *or* 60 g (2 oz) toasted pine nuts or walnuts

- ❏ Water

- ❏ **Before bed** – apply cream as directed, if necessary

DAY 10

Early morning

- ❏ **On waking** – a glass of hot water with a slice of lemon

- ❏ **Exercise** – 15 minutes of aerobic exercise

- ❏ **Before showering** – brush skin, particularly the areas affected by cellulite

- ❏ Shower or bath

- ❏ Apply cream etc.

Morning

- ❏ **Breakfast** – Slice of rye (or other non-wheat) bread or 3 rye crackers with a little olive oil spread and honey 125 g (4 oz) fresh fruit (e.g. apple, grapes, satsumas, grapefruit)

- ❏ Water

- ❏ **Mid-morning snack** – 125 g (4 oz) fresh fruit (e.g. strawberries, raspberries or blueberries)

- ❏ Water

Afternoon

- ❏ **Lunch** – Flageolet bean salad with peanuts (recipe page 96) 1 pot (150 g) plain soya or natural bio-yoghurt mixed with 1 tbsp (15 ml) muesli

- ❏ Water

- ❏ **Mid-afternoon snack** – 2 reduced-salt oatcakes topped with 2 tsp hummus

- ❏ Water

Evening

- ❏ **Exercise** – Lower body, middle body exercises plus complementary stretches. Repeat each exercise continuously for 30 seconds Use 2 kg hand weights or dumbbells for upper body exercises. After each exercise, the complementary stretch should be held for 30 seconds.

- ❏ **Dinner** – Pasta spirals with grilled vegetables (recipe page 98) Warm berry compote with cinnamon (recipe page 104)

- ❏ Water

- ❏ **Before bed** – apply cream as directed, if necessary

DAY 11

Early morning

- **On waking** – a glass of hot water with a slice of lemon

- **Exercise** – 15 minutes of aerobic exercise

- **Before showering** – brush skin, particularly the areas affected by cellulite

- Shower or bath

- Apply cream etc.

Morning

- **Breakfast** – Fruit and yoghurt (recipe page 85)

- Water

- **Mid-morning snack** – Smoothie (recipes pages 105–107)

- Water

Afternoon

- **Lunch** – Open sandwich made from 1 slice of rye bread (or other non-wheat bread, or 3 rye crispbreads) spread with hummus or guacamole (recipes page 94), sliced tomato and red peppers
  Mixed leaf salad with a drizzle of extra virgin olive oil and balsamic vinegar dressing
  125 g (4 oz) fresh fruit (e.g. apple, plums or banana)

- Water

- **Mid-afternoon snack** – Small handful of toasted seeds (e.g. pumpkin, sunflower or sesame seeds)

- Water

Evening

- **Exercise** – Upper body exercises plus complementary stretches. Repeat each exercise continuously for 30 seconds Use 2 kg hand weights or dumbbells. After each exercise, the complementary stretch should be held for 30 seconds.

- **Dinner** – Spiced beans with mushrooms and squash (recipe page 92)
  Salad leaves with balsamic dressing

- Water

- **Before bed** – apply cream as directed, if necessary

DAY 12

Early morning

- **On waking** – a glass of hot water with a slice of lemon

- **Exercise** – 15 minutes of aerobic exercise

- **Before showering** – brush skin, particularly the areas affected by cellulite

- Shower or bath

- Apply cream etc.

Morning

- **Breakfast** – 1 pot of plain soya yoghurt or natural bio-yoghurt mixed with 1 tsp (5 ml) clear honey and 125 g (4 oz) fresh fruit (e.g. banana, strawberries, nectarine or apple)

- Water

- **Mid-morning snack** – Celery, carrot and cucumber sticks dipped in a little hummus

- Water

Afternoon

- **Lunch** – Hummus (ready-made or recipe on page 94) Crudités (see page 93) Slice of rye (or other non-wheat) bread or 3 rye crackers with a little olive oil spread and honey 125 g (4 oz) fresh fruit (e.g. apple, grapes, satsumas, grapefruit)

- Water

- **Mid-afternoon snack** – Small handful of nuts (e.g. walnuts, almonds, or cashews) Water

Evening

- **Exercise** – Lower body, middle body exercises plus complementary stretches. Repeat each exercise continuously for 30 seconds. Use 2 kg hand weights or dumbbells for upper body exercises. After each exercise, the complementary stretch should be held for 30 seconds.

- **Dinner** – Penne with ratatouille (recipe page 101) 125 g (4 oz) steamed green vegetables (e.g. broccoli, cabbage, curly kale)

- Water

- **Before bed** – apply cream as directed, if necessary

DAY 13

Early morning

- ❏ **On waking** – a glass of hot water with a slice of lemon

- ❏ **Before showering** – brush skin, particularly the areas affected by cellulite

- ❏ Shower or bath

- ❏ Apply cream etc.

Morning

- ❏ **Breakfast** – Compote of dried fruit (recipe page 85)

- ❏ Water

- ❏ **Mid-morning snack** – 125 g (4 oz) fresh fruit (e.g. apple, pear or banana)

- ❏ Water

Afternoon

- ❏ **Lunch** – Spinach and courgette soup with toasted almonds (recipe page 82)
  Slice of rye (or other non-wheat) bread or 2 rye or rice crackers
  125 g (4 oz) fresh fruit (e.g. satsumas or clementines)

- ❏ Water

- ❏ **Mid-afternoon snack** – 2 reduced-salt oatcakes topped with 2 tsp hummus

- ❏ Water

Evening

- ❏ **Dinner** – Chickpeas with spinach and potato (recipe page 92)
  1 pot of plain soya yoghurt or natural bio-yoghurt mixed with 1 tsp (5 ml) clear honey

- ❏ Water

- ❏ **Before bed** – apply cream as directed, if necessary

DAY 14

Early morning

- ❏ **On waking** – a glass of hot water with a slice of lemon

- ❏ **Before showering** – brush skin, particularly the areas affected by cellulite

- ❏ Shower or bath

- ❏ Apply cream etc.

Morning

- ❏ **Breakfast** – Muesli with fruit and nuts (recipe page 84)

- ❏ Water

- ❏ **Mid-morning snack** – 1 pot plain soya yoghurt or natural bio-yoghurt mixed with 125 g (4 oz) chopped fresh fruit (e.g. strawberries, banana or blueberries)

- ❏ Water

Afternoon

- ❏ **Lunch** – Tomato and vegetable soup (recipe page 81)
  Slice of rye (or other non-wheat) bread or 2 rye or rice crackers
  125 g (4 oz) fresh fruit (e.g. kiwi fruit, satsumas or clementines)

- ❏ Water

- ❏ **Mid-afternoon snack** – 1 apple or pear

- ❏ Water

Evening

- ❏ **Dinner** – Noodle and tofu stir-fry (recipe page 101)
  Tropical fruit salad with honey and lime (recipe page 104)

- ❏ Water

- ❏ **Before bed** – apply cream as directed, if necessary

DAY 15

Early morning

- **On waking** – a glass of hot water with a slice of lemon

- **Exercise** – 15 minutes of aerobic exercise

- **Before showering** – brush skin, particularly the areas affected by cellulite

- Shower or bath

- Apply cream etc.

Morning

- **Breakfast** – Fruit and yoghurt (recipe page 85)

- Water

- **Mid-morning snack** – 4 brazil nuts

- Water

Afternoon

- **Lunch** – 1 small baked potato with a drizzle of extra virgin olive oil or flax seed oil
  1–2 tbsp (15–30 ml) hummus or guacamole (ready-bought or see recipes page 94)
  Mixed salad leaves
  125 g (4 oz) fresh fruit (e.g. peach, orange or kiwi fruit)

- Water

- **Mid-afternoon snack** – 1 apple or pear

- Water

Evening

- **Exercise** – Lower body exercises plus complementary stretches. Repeat each exercise continuously for 40 seconds and incorporate the use of ankle weights. After each exercise, the complementary stretch should be held for 30 seconds.

- **Dinner** – Grilled aubergines with mint and yoghurt dressing (recipe page 86)
  175 g (6 oz) steamed green vegetables (e.g. broccoli or Brussels sprouts)

- Water

- **Before bed** – apply cream as directed, if necessary

DAY 16 ••••

Early morning

- **On waking** – a glass of hot water with a slice of lemon

- **Exercise** – 15 minutes of aerobic exercise

- **Before showering** – brush skin, particularly the areas affected by cellulite

- Shower or bath

- Apply cream etc.

Morning

- **Breakfast** – Porridge with raisins and apricots (recipe page 84)

- Water

- **Mid-morning snack** – 125 g (4 oz) fresh fruit (e.g. peach, orange or kiwi fruit)

- Water

Afternoon

- **Lunch** – Salad leaves with fresh herbs and walnuts (recipe page 98)
  150g (5 oz) steamed or grilled cod steak *or* 60 g (2 oz) hummus
  125 g (4 oz) fresh fruit (e.g. melon, mango or red grapes)

- Water

- **Mid-afternoon snack** – Small handful of toasted seeds (e.g. pumpkin, sunflower or sesame seeds)

- Water

Evening

- **Exercise** – Upper body, middle body exercises plus complementary stretches. Repeat each exercise continuously for 40 seconds and incorporate the use of ankle weights. Use 3 kg hand weights or dumbbells for upper body exercises. After each exercise, the complementary stretch should be held for 30 seconds.

- **Dinner** – Roasted Mediterranean vegetables with olive and rosemary (recipe page 90)
  2 heaped tbsp (30 ml) cooked brown rice 85 g (3 oz) grilled white fish *or* 3 tbsp (45 ml) tinned beans (e.g. pinto beans, chickpeas)

- Water

- **Before bed** – apply cream as directed, if necessary

DAY 17

Early morning

- ❏ **On waking** – a glass of hot water with a slice of lemon

- ❏ **Exercise** – 15 minutes of aerobic exercise

- ❏ **Before showering** – brush skin, particularly the areas affected by cellulite

- ❏ Shower or bath

- ❏ Apply cream etc.

Morning

- ❏ **Breakfast** – Slice of rye (or other non-wheat) bread or 3 rye crackers with a little olive oil spread and honey 125 g (4 oz) fresh fruit (e.g. apple, grapes, satsumas, grapefruit)

- ❏ Water

- ❏ **Mid-morning snack** – 125 g (4 oz) fresh fruit (e.g. satsumas or clementines)

- ❏ Water

Afternoon

- ❏ **Lunch** – Hummus (ready-made or recipe on page 94) Crudités (see page 93) Slice of rye (or other non-wheat) bread or 3 rye crackers with a little olive oil spread and honey 125 g (4 oz) fresh fruit (e.g. apple, grapes or banana)

- ❏ Water

- ❏ **Mid-afternoon snack** – 2 reduced-salt oatcakes topped with 2 tsp hummus

- ❏ Water

Evening

- ❏ **Exercise** – Lower body, middle body exercises plus complementary stretches. Repeat each exercise continuously for 40 seconds and incorporate the use of ankle weights. Use 3 kg hand weights or dumbbells for upper body exercises. After each exercise, the complementary stretch should be held for 30 seconds.

- ❏ **Dinner** – Lentil dahl with fresh coriander (recipe page 93) 2 heaped tbsp (30 ml) cooked brown rice 225 g (8 oz) steamed vegetables (e.g. carrots, broccoli, courgettes, green beans)

- ❏ Water

- ❏ **Before bed** – apply cream as directed, if necessary

DAY 18

Early morning

- ❏ **On waking** – a glass of hot water with a slice of lemon

- ❏ **Exercise** – 15 minutes of aerobic exercise

- ❏ **Before showering** – brush skin, particularly the areas affected by cellulite

- ❏ Shower or bath

- ❏ Apply cream etc.

Morning

- ❏ **Breakfast** – 225 g (8 oz) mixture of fresh fruit (e.g. melon, grapefruit, oranges, peaches, strawberries, kiwi fruit) 1–2 tbsp (15–30 ml) nuts (e.g. toasted almonds, hazelnuts or cashews)

- ❏ Water

- ❏ **Mid-morning snack** – 2 rice crackers (rice cakes) topped with 2 tsp (10 ml) peanut butter

- ❏ Water

Afternoon

- ❏ **Lunch** – Open sandwich made from 1 slice of rye bread (or other non-wheat bread, or 3 rye crispbreads) with 100 g (3½ oz) drained tuna in spring water mixed with a little lemon juice *or* 2 tbsp (30 ml) hummus (recipe pages 94) Mixed leaf salad with a drizzle of extra virgin olive oil and balsamic vinegar dressing 125 g (4 oz) fresh fruit (e.g. apple, plums or banana)

- ❏ Water

- ❏ **Mid afternoon snack** – 1 pot plain soya yoghurt or natural bio-yoghurt mixed with 1 tbsp chopped toasted nuts (e.g. almonds, hazelnuts or walnuts)

- ❏ Water

Evening

- ❏ **Exercise** – Upper body exercises plus complementary stretches. Repeat each exercise continuously for 40 seconds. Use 3 kg hand weights or dumbbells. After each exercise, the complementary stretch should be held for 30 seconds.

- ❏ **Dinner** – Pasta spirals with grilled vegetables (recipe page 98) Raspberry tofu cream (recipe page 102)

- ❏ Water

- ❏ **Before bed** – apply cream as directed, if necessary

DAY 19

Early morning

- **On waking** – a glass of hot water with a slice of lemon

- **Exercise** – 15 minutes of aerobic exercise

- **Before showering** – brush skin, particularly the areas affected by cellulite

- Shower or bath

- Apply cream etc.

Morning

- **Breakfast** – Fruit and yoghurt (recipe page 85)

- Water

- **Mid-morning snack** – 1 pot plain soya yoghurt or natural bio-yoghurt mixed with 3 chopped dried apricots

- Water

Afternoon

- **Lunch** – Half an avocado
  Mixed salad of salad leaves, tomato, yellow pepper and radish
  85 (3 oz) cooked peeled prawns *or* 2 tbsp (30 ml) hummus

- Water

- **Mid-afternoon snack** – 125 g (4 oz) fresh fruit (e.g. oranges, satsumas, kiwi fruit)

- Water

Evening

- **Exercise** – Lower body, middle body exercises plus complementary stretches. Repeat each exercise continuously for 40 seconds and incorporate the use of ankle weights. Use 3 kg hand weights or dumbbells for upper body exercises. After each exercise, the complementary stretch should be held for 30 seconds.

- **Dinner** – Stir-fried vegetables with cashews (recipe page 86)
  125 g (4 oz) stir-fried tofu
  2 heaped tbsp (30 ml) cooked brown rice

- Water

- **Before bed** – apply cream as directed, if necessary

DAY 20

Early morning

- **On waking** – a glass of hot water with a slice of lemon

- **Before showering** – brush skin, particularly the areas affected by cellulite

- Shower or bath

- Apply cream etc.

Morning

- **Breakfast** – Muesli with fruit and nuts (recipe page 84)

- Water

- **Mid-morning snack** – Smoothie (recipes pages 105–107)

- Water

Afternoon

- **Lunch** – Warm chickpea salad with green beans and cashews (recipe page 96)
125 g (4 oz) fresh fruit (e.g. oranges, satsumas, kiwi fruit)

- Water

- **Mid-afternoon snack** – Small handful of nuts (e.g. walnuts, almonds or cashews)

- Water

Evening

- **Dinner** – Rice noodles with vegetables in spiced coconut milk (recipe page 97)
1 pot (150 ml) plain soya yoghurt or natural bio-yoghurt mixed with 1 tbsp (15 ml) raisins or apricots

- Water

- **Before bed** – apply cream as directed, if necessary

DAY 21

Early morning

- ❏ **On waking** – a glass of hot water with a slice of lemon

- ❏ **Before showering** – brush skin, particularly the areas affected by cellulite

- ❏ Shower or bath

- ❏ Apply cream etc.

Morning

- ❏ **Breakfast** – Compote of dried fruit (recipe page 85)

- ❏ Water

- ❏ **Mid-morning snack** – 125 g (4 oz) fresh fruit (e.g. satsumas or clementines)

- ❏ Water

Afternoon

- ❏ **Lunch** – Spinach and courgette soup with toasted almonds (recipe page 82)
Slice of rye (or other non-wheat) bread or 2 rye or rice crackers
125 g (4 oz) fresh fruit (e.g. strawberries, raspberries or blueberries)

- ❏ Water

- ❏ **Mid-afternoon snack** – Small handful of toasted seeds (e.g. pumpkin, sunflower or sesame)

- ❏ Water

Evening

- ❏ **Dinner** – Roasted root vegetables (recipe page 90)
100 g (3¹/₂ oz) poached salmon *or* 60 g (2 oz) toasted pine nuts or walnuts
Fresh fruit with honey (recipe page 102)

- ❏ Water

- ❏ **Before bed** – apply cream as directed, if necessary

DAY 22

Early morning

- ❏ **On waking** – a glass of hot water with a slice of lemon

- ❏ **Exercise** – 15 minutes of aerobic exercise

- ❏ **Before showering** – brush skin, particularly the areas affected by cellulite

- ❏ Shower or bath

- ❏ Apply cream etc.

Morning

- ❏ **Breakfast** – Porridge with raisins and apricots (recipe page 84)

- ❏ Water

- ❏ **Mid-morning snack** – Smoothie (recipes pages 105–107)

- ❏ Water

Afternoon

- ❏ **Lunch** – Hummus (ready-made or recipe on page 94)
  Crudités (see page 93)
  Slice of rye (or other non-wheat) bread or 3 rye crackers with a little olive oil spread and honey
  125 g (4 oz) fresh fruit (e.g. apple, grapes, satsumas, grapefruit)

- ❏ Water

- ❏ **Mid-afternoon snack** – Small handful of nuts (e.g. walnuts, almonds or cashews)

- ❏ Water

Evening

- ❏ **Exercise** – Lower body exercises plus complementary stretches. Repeat each exercise continuously for 50 seconds and incorporate the use of ankle weights. After each exercise, the complementary stretch should be held for 30 seconds.

- ❏ **Dinner** – Spiced beans with mushrooms and squash (recipe page 92)
  Salad leaves with balsamic dressing

- ❏ Water

- ❏ **Before bed** – apply cream as directed, if necessary

DAY 23

Early morning

- ❑ **On waking** – a glass of hot water with a slice of lemon

- ❑ **Exercise** – 15 minutes of aerobic exercise

- ❑ **Before showering** – brush skin, particularly the areas affected by cellulite

- ❑ Shower or bath

- ❑ Apply cream etc.

Morning

- ❑ **Breakfast** – Fruit and yoghurt (recipe page 85)

- ❑ Water

- ❑ **Mid-morning snack** – 60 g (2 oz) dried fruit (e.g. apricots, prunes, peaches or mango)

- ❑ Water

Afternoon

- ❑ **Lunch** – 1 small baked potato with a drizzle of extra virgin olive oil or flax seed oil
  225 g (8 oz) steamed vegetables (e.g. carrots, broccoli, cabbage or cauliflower)
  A few walnuts or flaked almonds
  125 g (4 oz) fresh fruit (e.g. peach, orange or kiwi fruit)

- ❑ Water

- ❑ **Mid-afternoon snack** – 1 pot plain soya yoghurt or natural bio-yoghurt

- ❑ Water

Evening

- ❑ **Exercise** – Upper body, middle body exercises plus complementary stretches. Repeat each exercise continuously for 50 seconds and incorporate the use of ankle weights. Use 3 kg hand weights or dumbbells for upper body exercises. After each exercise, the complementary stretch should be held for 30 seconds.

- ❑ **Dinner** – Pasta with spring vegetables (recipe page 97)
  1 pot plain soya or natural bio-yoghurt mixed with 2 tbsp berries (e.g. strawberries, raspberries or blueberries)

- ❑ Water

- ❑ **Before bed** – apply cream as directed, if necessary

DAY 24

Early morning

- **On waking** – a glass of hot water with a slice of lemon

- **Exercise** – 15 minutes of aerobic exercise

- **Before showering** – brush skin, particularly the areas affected by cellulite

- Shower or bath

- Apply cream etc.

Morning

- **Breakfast** – 225 g (8 oz) mixture of fresh fruit (e.g. melon, grapefruit, oranges, peaches, strawberries, kiwi fruit) 1–2 tbsp (15–30 ml) nuts (e.g. toasted almonds, hazelnuts or cashews)

- Water

- **Mid-morning snack** – 125 g (4 oz) fresh fruit (e.g. satsumas or clementines)

- Water

Afternoon

- **Lunch** – Romaine salad with honey and mustard dressing (recipe page 95) Slice of rye (or other non-wheat) bread or 2 rye or rice crackers Fresh fruit with honey (recipe page 102)

- Water

- **Mid-afternoon snack** – 2 rice crackers (rice cakes) topped with 2 tsp (10 ml) peanut butter

- Water

Evening

- **Exercise** – Lower body, middle body exercises plus complementary stretches. Repeat each exercise continuously for 50 seconds and incorporate the use of ankle weights. Use 3 kg hand weights or dumbbells for upper body exercises. After each exercise, the complementary stretch should be held for 30 seconds.

- **Dinner** – 2 heaped tbsp (30 ml) cooked brown rice Spinach with pine nuts (recipe page 89) Salad leaves with a little balsamic dressing

- Water

- **Before bed** – apply cream as directed, if necessary

DAY 25

Early morning

- ❏ **On waking** – a glass of hot water with a slice of lemon

- ❏ **Exercise** – 15 minutes of aerobic exercise

- ❏ **Before showering** – brush skin, particularly the areas affected by cellulite

- ❏ Shower or bath

- ❏ Apply cream etc.

Morning

- ❏ **Breakfast** – Strawberry smoothie (recipe page 107) Small handful of nuts (e.g. walnuts, almonds) or seeds (e.g. pumpkin seeds, sunflower seeds)

- ❏ Water

- ❏ **Mid-morning snack** – 125 g (4 oz) fresh fruit (e.g. satsumas or clementines)

- ❏ Water

Afternoon

- ❏ **Lunch** – Carrot soup with fresh coriander (recipe page 81) Slice of rye (or other non-wheat) bread or 2 rye or rice crackers 125 g (4 oz) fresh fruit (e.g. plums, peach or nectarine)

- ❏ Water

- ❏ **Mid-afternoon snack** – 1 pot of plain soya yoghurt or natural bio-yoghurt yoghurt mixed with 1 tsp (5 ml) clear honey

- ❏ Water

Evening

- ❏ **Exercise** – upper body exercises plus complementary stretches. Repeat each exercise continuously for 50 seconds. Use 3 kg hand weights or dumbbells. After each exercise, the complementary stretch should be held for 30 seconds.

- ❏ **Dinner** – Quinoa and rice with pumpkin seeds (recipe page 89) Fruit jelly (recipe page 104)

- ❏ Water

- ❏ **Before bed** – apply cream as directed, if necessary

DAY 26

Early morning

- ❑ **On waking** – a glass of hot water with a slice of lemon

- ❑ **Exercise** – 15 minutes of aerobic exercise

- ❑ **Before showering** – brush skin, particularly the areas affected by cellulite

- ❑ Shower or bath

- ❑ Apply cream etc.

Morning

- ❑ **Breakfast** – Compote of dried fruit (recipe page 85)

- ❑ Water

- ❑ **Mid-morning snack** – Smoothie (recipes, pages 105–107)

- ❑ Water

Afternoon

- ❑ **Lunch** – Open sandwich made from 1 slice of rye bread (or other non-wheat bread, or 3 rye crispbreads) with 85 g (3 oz) grilled chicken or turkey *or* 2 tbsp (30 ml) hummus and sliced tomato
  Mixed leaf salad with a drizzle of extra virgin olive oil and balsamic vinegar dressing
  125 g (4 oz) fresh fruit (e.g. apple, plums or banana)

- ❑ Water

- ❑ **Mid-afternoon snack** – Small handful of nuts (e.g. walnuts, almonds or cashews)

- ❑ Water

Evening

- ❑ **Exercise** – Lower body, middle body exercises plus complementary stretches. Repeat each exercise continuously for 50 seconds and incorporate the use of ankle weights. After each exercise, the complementary stretch should be held for 30 seconds.

- ❑ **Dinner** – Penne with ratatouille (recipe page 101)
  125 g (4 oz) steamed green vegetables (e.g. broccoli, cabbage, curly kale)

- ❑ Water

- ❑ **Before bed** – apply cream as directed, if necessary

DAY 27 ● ● ● ●

Early morning

- **On waking** – a glass of hot water with a slice of lemon

- **Before showering** – brush skin, particularly the areas affected by cellulite

- Shower or bath

- Apply cream etc.

Morning

- **Breakfast** – Muesli with fruit and nuts (recipe page 84)

- Water

- **Mid-morning snack** – 125 g (4 oz) fresh fruit (e.g. mango, apricots or nectarine)

- Water

Afternoon

- **Lunch** – Guacamole (ready-made or recipe on page 94) Crudités (see page 93) Slice of rye (or other non-wheat) bread or 3 rye crackers with a little olive oil spread and honey 125 g (4 oz) fresh fruit (e.g. apple, grapes, satsumas, grapefruit)

- Water

- **Mid-afternoon snack** – Small handful of toasted seeds (e.g. pumpkin, sunflower or sesame seeds)

- Water

Evening

- **Dinner** – 125 g (4 oz) grilled sardines (or other oily fish) *or* 125 g (4 oz) tinned beans (e.g. chickpeas, red kidney beans) 225 g (8 oz) steamed vegetables (e.g. broccoli, Brussels sprouts, cauliflower, carrots) Warm berry compote with cinnamon (recipe page 105)

- Water

- **Before bed** – apply cream as directed, if necessary

DAY 28

Early morning

- **On waking** – a glass of hot water with a slice of lemon

- **Before showering** – brush skin, particularly the areas affected by cellulite

- Shower or bath

- Apply cream etc.

Morning

- **Breakfast** – Porridge with raisins and apricots (recipe page 84)

- Water

- **Mid-morning snack** – 125 g (4 oz) fresh fruit (e.g. peach, orange or kiwi fruit)

- Water

Afternoon

- **Lunch** – Spinach, rocket and avocado salad (recipe page 95) 1 slice of rye bread (or other non-wheat bread, or 3 rye crispbreads) with a little olive oil spread 125 g (4 oz) fresh fruit (e.g. grapes, melon or banana)

- Water

- **Mid-afternoon snack** – Small handful of toasted seeds (e.g. pumpkin, sunflower or sesame seeds)

- Water

Evening

- **Dinner** – Chickpeas with spinach and potato (recipe page 92) 1 pot of plain soya yoghurt or natural bio-yoghurt mixed with 1 tsp (5 ml) clear honey

- Water

- **Before bed** – apply cream as directed, if necessary

DAY 29

Early morning

- ❏ **On waking** – a glass of hot water with a slice of lemon

- ❏ **Exercise** – 15 minutes of aerobic exercise

- ❏ **Before showering** – brush skin, particularly the areas affected by cellulite

- ❏ Shower or bath

- ❏ Apply cream etc.

Morning

- ❏ **Breakfast** – Mango and orange smoothie (recipe page 106) Small handful of nuts (e.g. walnuts, almonds) or seeds (e.g. pumpkin seeds, sunflower seeds)

- ❏ Water

- ❏ **Mid-morning snack** – 4 brazil nuts

- ❏ Water

Afternoon

- ❏ **Lunch** – 1 small baked potato with a drizzle of extra virgin olive oil or flax seed oil
225 g (8 oz) steamed vegetables (e.g. carrots, broccoli, cabbage or cauliflower)
1 pot plain soya yoghurt or natural bio-yoghurt mixed with 125 g (4 oz) chopped fresh fruit (e.g. strawberries, banana or blueberries)

- ❏ Water

- ❏ **Mid-afternoon snack** – 125 g (4 oz) fresh fruit (e.g. mango, apricots or nectarine)

- ❏ Water

Evening

- ❏ **Exercise** – Lower body exercises plus complementary stretches. Repeat each exercise continuously for 60 seconds and incorporate the use of ankle weights. After each exercise, the complementary stretch should be held for 30 seconds.

- ❏ **Dinner** – Flageolet bean salad with peanuts (recipe page 96) Salad leaves
Raspberry tofu cream (recipe page 102)

- ❏ Water

- ❏ **Before bed** – apply cream as directed, if necessary

DAY 30

Early morning

- ❏ **On waking** – a glass of hot water with a slice of lemon

- ❏ **Exercise** – 15 minutes of aerobic exercise

- ❏ **Before showering** – brush skin, particularly the areas affected by cellulite

- ❏ Shower or bath

- ❏ Apply cream etc.

Morning

- ❏ **Breakfast** – Fruit and yoghurt (recipe page 85)

- ❏ Water

- ❏ **Mid-morning snack** – 2 rice crackers (rice cakes) topped with 2 tsp (10 ml) peanut butter

- ❏ Water

Afternoon

- ❏ **Lunch** – Hummus (ready-made or recipe on page 94)
  Crudités (see page 93)
  Slice of rye (or other non-wheat) bread or 3 rye crackers with a little olive oil spread and honey
  125 g (4 oz) fresh fruit (e.g. apple, grapes, satsumas, grapefruit)

- ❏ Water

- ❏ **Mid-afternoon snack** – 60 g (2 oz) dried fruit (e.g. prunes, mango, apricots or apples)

- ❏ Water

Evening

- ❏ **Exercise** – Upper body exercises plus complementary stretches. Repeat each exercise continuously for 60 seconds. Use 3 kg hand weights or dumbbells. After each exercise, the complementary stretch should be held for 30 seconds.

- ❏ **Dinner** – Noodle and tofu stir-fry (recipe page 101)
  Fresh fruit with honey (recipe page 102)

- ❏ Water

- ❏ **Before bed** – apply cream as directed, if necessary

CHAPTER 5
HOME TREATMENTS

The 30-Day Plan doesn't just involve diet and exercise. It also recommends the use of a treatment that you can use at home and you will be pleased to know that there's plenty you can do that doesn't cost a great deal to help fight cellulite. Five or ten minutes in the bathroom every day can certainly help the appearance of your skin and make those cellulite dimples look less prominent.

If you do have cash to spare, you'll probably be tempted by many of the cellulite beauty treatments available. While the jury's still out on exactly how effective they really are, some ingredients do have impressive results. Pampering can also be good for your self-esteem because it's devoting time for yourself. So it can mean you're more likely to maintain your anti-cellulite regime and it all goes towards helping make it a more pleasant and indulgent experience.

Dry skin brushing

This plays a role in helping to beat cellulite because it's said to stimulate circulation and the lymphatic flow. Plus it can help make your skin softer as well as look and feel more even-textured because it removes dead surface skin cells. It's also thought to encourage new skin cells to regenerate and boost collagen production.

HOW TO DO IT?
The best tools for this are either a loofah or a body brush with very firm natural fibres – they're gentler than man-made fibres (and you can find them relatively easily in the high street in shops such as the Body Shop and Boots). Brush your skin every day before your shower or bath. But brush slowly and gently – in long strokes towards the heart. It should take no more than about three to five minutes – and doing it in the morning is a good way to start the day because it's invigorating.

TRY THIS STEP-BY-STEP ROUTINE:
1 Start at your feet. Put the brush against the sole of your left foot and brush gently but firmly with several rhythmic strokes in upward movements. Brush your toes, too, then brush the top of your foot, again always using an upward motion, towards your ankle. Brush the front and back of your lower legs up towards your groin. Repeat on your right foot and lower leg.
2 Move up to your thighs. Rest your left foot against the bath or a chair and brush the area from your knee to the top of your thigh. Use long, smooth, strokes, up over your buttocks towards your waist. Repeat on your right thigh.
3 This is trickier, but try brushing in several upward motions from your buttocks up to your shoulders.
4 Then focus on your arms. Start at your wrist and brush the inner arm in upward strokes towards your elbow. Then brush the palm of your hand and move up towards the back of your arm. Repeat on the other arm. Make sure you cover every inch of skin.
5 Then brush your abdomen using very gently circular movements – in a clockwise direction. Use very light pressure on this sensitive area.
6 Finally, brush your neck and chest – go gently in these areas, too – always remembering to move in the direction of your heart.
7 Then have a bath or shower to remove the dead skin cells. Wash your brush every few weeks with shampoo or warm water and leave it to dry.

Self massage

Beauty experts say that regular manual lymphatic drainage is a good way to help beat cellulite because it helps reduce fluid retention. You can also give yourself a mini-massage at home. Massaging areas of your skin regularly – even for a few minutes a day – can help improve blood flow and lymphatic circulation and moisturise your skin.

WHAT TO USE?

Any good moisturising cream or lotion will do. Try a carrier oil/aromatherapy solution (see opposite), or experiment with any of the many cellulite products available (see page 70). Anything that helps your hands glide over your body and feels lovely and moisturising.

As well as helping boost circulation, massaging your skin helps hydrate it; when your skin is dry and dehydrated, cellulite appears far more noticeable. When you moisturise your skin, you're effectively plumping it up, helping to smooth out some of those dimples.

Try this 3–4-minute legs, tums and bums self-massage treatment every day, as prescribed by Emma Maclennan, Assistant Training Manager at Decléor UK; they use similar techniques during their salon treatments.

You can use this method to apply your aromatherapy oils, or rich moisturising cream. Aim to give yourself a mini-massage, ideally after a bath or shower, every morning, and always before you go to bed at night.

1   Start by relaxing – taking a few deep breaths in for the count of four, and then out for the count of four – so you also relax the muscles. If you're using an aromatherapy-based treatment, inhale the oils.

2   Rub your hands together to warm the lotion/oil and make it easier to apply.

3   Start with your thighs. Use a gentle but firm upwards stroke, going towards the top of the leg from the knee. Always work upwards, towards the heart, so you're working *with* the circulation and lymphatic flow.

4   Then, using loose fingers, gently 'knead' the thighs as if you were kneading dough. Move around your thigh, from outside to inside.

5   Move to your buttock areas. Place the palms of your hands flat on your buttocks and circle upwards and outwards, one hand on each buttock. Again, use long, gentle movements.

6   Next, massage your stomach. Use gentle circular movements with the flats of your hands.

7   Finally, move to your arms. Work your way upwards from your wrist towards your shoulder, using a firm, but gentle kneading movement. Then glide down your arm again to your wrist. Repeat several times on each arm.

Essential oils

Aromatherapy is another tool that can help fight cellulite. Essential oils have various therapeutic properties that have been found to have physical and mental effects. They are used by aromatherapists to treat everything, from tension headaches to eczema, insomnia and acne.

You can use them in various ways: massage with them, add drops to your bath, pop them on a tissue and smell them, or burn them in a diffuser and inhale the scent.

HOW DO THEY WORK?

They're absorbed by the skin when applied topically and then absorbed into your body's circulatory system. When you inhale them, for example, they're passed through the blood stream via the lungs. And when you smell the various odours they trigger a series of messages, which reach your brain.

The best essential oils for helping beat cellulite are those with diuretic qualities (which means they can help beat water retention), those that can help boost the circulation and get the lymphatic system working more efficiently and those that can help suppress your appetite, or regulate your hormones (oestrogen is linked with cellulite). Some essential oils have uplifting, energising properties – which can encourage you to take more exercise! Some are good for your skin itself, and, if you apply them topically within a carrier oil, you get the added benefit of moisturising the skin on your cellulite areas, too.

Make sure you get advice from an aromatherapist because some oils have contraindications during pregnancy and with certain medical conditions such as diabetes, epilepsy and kidney problems.

THE BEST CELLULITE-BUSTING ESSENTIAL OILS

Rosemary: This minty/herbal oil has purifying qualities, and also helps alleviate water retention. It's also known for its astringent action, so it can help to tighten sagging skin – another plus for fighting cellulite. It's invigorating and stimulating, too, so try burning it or sniffing it; it could put you in the mood for some exercise! Avoid during pregnancy, if you're epileptic or have high blood pressure.

Atlas Cedarwood: This lovely, woody smelling oil is said to encourage lymphatic drainage and to help stimulate the breakdown of fats. It also has a diuretic action so it can help alleviate fluid retention. It's known for its calming and soothing effects, so can help you stay focused on your anti-cellulite plan! It's best avoided during pregnancy.

Grapefruit: This is rich in vitamin C, so it's good for your skin. It's a lymphatic stimulant, which helps with fluid retention. It's thought to help with fat digestion, because of its stimulating effect on bile. It's also good for stress, but can be an appetite suppressant. However, it is enlivening so you may feel more like exercising after inhaling this.

Cypress: A refreshing fragrance, this is known for its regulating effects on the body's fluids. It's good for your circulation, too, and has a balancing effect on female hormones, which can also help beat cellulite. It can also help balance fluid loss, so it keeps more mature skin looking and feeling better hydrated. Avoid using during pregnancy.

Sweet fennel: Smells aniseedy and peppery, and is known for its cleansing and tonic action. It's good for your digestive system and has diuretic properties so can help with water retention. It could possibly stimulate your appetite, so keep the biscuit tin hidden – but it has positive, balancing effects on oestrogen (the hormone linked with cellulite). It can also tone saggy, wrinkly skin. Best avoided if you're pregnant or epileptic.

Juniper: A good detoxifier, which helps regulate your appetite. It helps to relieve fluid retention, and can be stimulating and refreshing. Avoid during pregnancy or if you have kidney problems. Large quantities can irritate the skin.

Geranium: This has a lovely sweet smell, and is a great circulation booster. It's good for fluid retention, and can help balance your hormone levels. It helps your immune system, too. Add it to your bath – it's a good stress buster, so can help reduce stress-induced binges!

Patchouli: A strong, spicy oil, this has diuretic properties so it's good for fluid retention. It's also known for its positive effects on the skin, encouraging the growth of new skin cells, which can help improve cellulite areas. It can also help curb your appetite, and is uplifting so it motivates you in your anti-cellulite programme.

AROMATHERAPY CELLULITE BUSTERS

When using essential oils in the bath, just add four to six drops of oil to your bath. Add milk or a drop of vodka to help the oil to disperse, as neat oils can irritate your skin.

Anti-cellulite bath: Add two drops each of cypress, lavender and lemon oils to your bath. Sit and relax for ten minutes. Then have a cold shower, and rub an oil made from mixing 10 ml (2 tsp) soya oil, two drops of wheatgerm oil and seven drops of cypress oil into the affected areas.

For massage: You can make your own massage oil by mixing six drops of essential oils to about 3–4 tsp (15–20 ml) of carrier oil. (Don't use essential oils neat on the skin as they can cause irritation.) The best carrier oils to use include sweet almond oil, which is good for dry, wrinkled or sensitive skin and is rich in skin-boosting vitamins. Grapeseed oil is another good choice, as it's well absorbed by your skin.

Try this home-made anti-cellulite massage oil: mix together 15 ml (1 tbsp) almond oil, two drops of wheatgerm oil, eight drops of cumin oil, two or three drops of orange or lemon oil, and use to massage your legs, thighs and tummy areas. Massage it in to the affected areas gently but firmly, as if you were kneading dough.

Shelving out: beauty creams

Walk into any beauty store or high-street chemist and you'll be faced with shelf upon shelf of beautifully packaged unguents, all claiming they can help you beat cellulite. Most manufacturers acknowledge that their product should be used alongside a healthy, low fat diet and regular exercise rather than be used in isolation like some kind of miracle fat and dimple eraser. Plus, you usually need to use them for a minimum of 30 days twice a day to see any results. Always read the small print on the products' labels.

So do they actually work? The jury's out on this one. Although many of the products come with details of studies showing that they can help alleviate dimpling as well as reduce inches, experts do concur that you would need to adopt a lifestyle approach to get lasting improvement.

However, cellulite creams can certainly help hydrate the area – and anything that helps firm and plump up the skin can help the appearance of dimply skin. And as some of our illustrations show, this can happen. Plus, there are other ingredients that do seem to have a positive effect on the dimples and pitted skin that characterise cellulite.

COMMON INGREDIENTS IN CELLULITE CREAMS:

Aminophylline: This substance is derived from theophylline, which is traditionally used by doctors to relax certain types of muscles such as the lungs. It's best known as an asthma medication. Some experts claim it can enter fat cells and break down fat. In one study women lost 8 mm around their legs after using aminophylline cream. Although another study contradicted the findings by proving the cream can't actually enter the bloodstream, the debate continues. In another study patients applied aminophylline, and also ate a calorie-reduced diet and exercised every day; they also reported a reduction in their cellulite. More research is needed, so watch this space.

Retinol: You'll probably be familiar with this, and may already use a face cream that contains this derivative of vitamin A. Retinol increases skin renewal, and boosts the production of collagen, which improves the elasticity of the skin. Retinol-based creams should really only be used at night, as retinol is destroyed when exposed to light.

AHAs (Alpha Hydroxy Acids): AHAs are found in plants such as citrus fruits and apples, and are used in skin products to work as an exfoliator, helping to remove dead skin cells and assisting the turnover of cells. They may work by temporarily tightening the skin on cellulite areas but there is no research yet which has found any really lasting results.

Gotu Kola: This herb contains substances known as triterpenes, which are thought to enhance the production of collagen. It can also help keep blood vessels strong and boost circulation, plus it has diuretic qualities. In one study, patients who took gotu kola internally reported a 58 per cent reduction in their cellulite. Used topically, it's been found to help heal wounds and burns, so has positive effects on healing skin tissue.

Caffeine: Although drinking caffeine seems to exacerbate cellulite – because it can dehydrate you – when used topically in cellulite creams it's thought to work by helping release fat from fat cells and boosting the circulation. It is also toning.

Horse Chestnut (*aesculus hippocastanum*): This plant can help reduce water retention and boost circulation in your legs, which can increase blood flow to the skin.

Butcher's Broom (*ruscus aculeatus*): Studies have shown that this plant extract can help boost circulation and has a diuretic action.

Ivy (*hedera helix*): This has been found to have anti-inflammatory effects, and can help boost the circulation. It also has astringent properties, which may help tone the cellulitey areas – at least temporarily.

Guarana: This seed has a strong diuretic action (it contains caffeine) and is a stimulant, which may play a role in boosting metabolism. It also has antioxidant qualities.

Gingko biloba: This has been found to help dilate the capillaries which means it can stimulate your circulation and boost blood flow. It also has strong antioxidant properties, so it may help slow down the ageing process and help fight the free radicals that can cause your skin to sag and wrinkle.

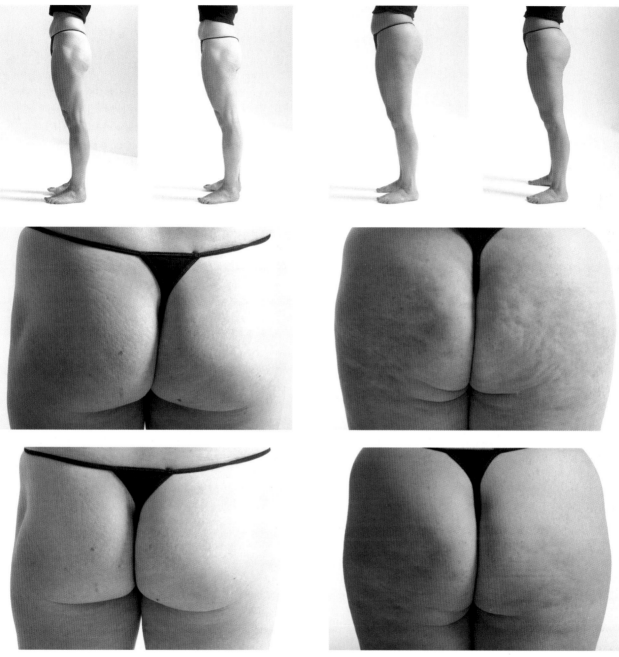

- **Age:** 42
- Used Vichy's Liposyne Body Contouring Treatment with
  Adrenalyse for 30 days but did not follow the plan
- **Total weight loss:** 4 lb (1.7 kg) due to other factors
  – 13 st 4 lb (84.5 kg) to 12 st 11 lb (80.4 kg)
- **Total inch loss:** 12 in (30 cm)

- **Age:** 29
- Diet, exercise and Marks & Spencer's Body Formula
  Cellulite Control Treatment and Massager
- **Total weight loss:** 6 lb (2.5 kg)
  – 8 st 10 lb (55 kg) to 8 st 4 lb (52.5 kg)
- **Total inch loss:** 9 in (22.5 cm)

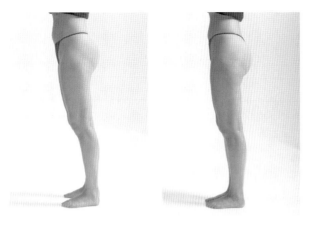

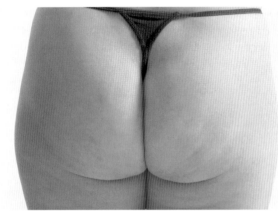

- **Age:** 33
- Diet, exercise and Germaine de Capuccini Perfect Forms Patch Contour & Ampoules
- **Total weight loss:** 5 lb (2.3 kg) due to other factors
  – 9 st 5 lb (59.5 kg) to 9 st (57.2 kg)
- **Total inch loss:** 6 in (15 cm)

Here are a few of the products available on the high street today, which we tested. Here's a quick guide to what they offer:

* Dior's Bikini Celluli-Diet Body Refining Essence, £29

What they say: In trials, women noticed an 89 per cent reduction in cellulite after a month of using this refreshing spray-on lotion twice a day. Its key ingredient anogelline is said to stop the breakdown of the skin's support tissue. Also contains an aromacology-based fragrance, said to help suppress your appetite, too – the essential oils apparently help stop you nibbling!

* Vichy Liposyne Body Contouring Treatment with Adrenalyse, £19.95

What they say: This contains a new formulation – known as adrenalyse complex – a mixture of vegetable extracts and caffeine, which is said to help stimulate fatty deposits. In four-week studies, women said their skin became 30 per cent smoother and 20 per cent less dimply. Ideally, use it in conjunction with their recommended 'micro-massage' technique – massage each thigh with both hands, in an upward motion, from your knees to your buttock.

* Marks & Spencer Body Formula Cellulite Control Treatment, £9, and Cellulite Massager, £7

What they say: You use this cooling gel in conjunction with the cellulite massager. In studies, testers noticed their thighs were 70 per cent firmer after using for a month.

Estée Lauder Body Performance Anti-Cellulite Visible Contouring Serum, £28, Firming Body Crème £29, and Exfoliating Body Polish, £24

What they say: That their testers lost up to 2.4 cm from their thighs in four weeks using this blue menthol-smelling lotion. Its unique ingredient formulation is the Thermogenic Complex, which contains natural ingredients to help melt away fatty deposits.

* Yves Saint Laurent Total Fitness Ultra-Silky Slimming Gel, £28.50

What they say: It contains a floral gel with a powerful new ingredient extracted from a Californian bush, which is said to help block the multiplication of fat cells. Two months' use could apparently help eliminate 560,000 fat cells from your thighs (making them about 5.6 per cent smaller)! And in their trials, 68 per cent of testers noticed an improvement in their orange peel skin.

* **Décleor Aromessence Contour, £33.50, Expert Contour, £31.50, Aromessence Baume Contour, £33**

What they say: Your thighs could get up to 1.5 cm slimmer in four weeks using this gorgeous-smelling trio of aromatherapy-based products. Plus when you inhale the essential oils in these products, it apparently activates a 'fat-eating' protein to help whittle away your wobbly bits!

* **Elancyl Lipo-Reducing Concentrate, £19.95**

What they say: That it contains active ingredients such as caffeine and 'draining ingredients' and that, in their studies, 81 per cent of participants noticed firmer skin and a loss of 2.9 cm from their thighs after using every day for fourteen days.

* **Roc Retinol Body Modelling, £21.95**

What they say: That it contains vitamin A (retinol) which helps reduce fat storage and stimulates cell renewal, which can smooth the surface of the skin and reduce the dimples. It also has an ingredient which gives a quick, albeit temporary, firming effect too. In eight weeks 72.5 per cent of their testers noticed a reduction in their thighs – by up to 4.8 cm.

* **L'Oréal Paris Perfectslim Anti-cellulite + Firming body gel, £10.99, L'Oréal Paris Perfectslim Night Body refining anti-cellulite gel, £10.99**

What they say: That it reduces the circumference of women's thighs by up to 2 cm in fourteen days.

* **Clarins Body Firming Cream, £28.50**

What they say: Helps to reduce the appearance of cellulite if used regularly and has a firming effect on the skin.

* **Germaine de Capuccini Perfect Forms Patch Countour, £59.50 (*www.germaine-de-capuccini.co.uk*)**

These patches, which originate from Spain, are transparent adhesive patches that you stick over the affected areas, and wear for 24 hours like a sticking plaster. They are said to work by delivering a 'constant' supply of cellulite busting ingredients such as algae, which helps boost metabolism, stimulate the elimination of toxins and help to smooth and firm the skin. Each pack contains an intensive fifteen-day treatment.

* **Germaine De Capuccini Perfect Forms Reduce Zone Cellulite Ampoules, £39.55**

(*see above for stockist details*)

Among the ingredients in these are aescin, phyco-75 and algisium C. They come in packs lasting fifteen days and are said to block fat accumulation, boost circulation and help with the elimination of fat, water and toxins.

It would have been impossible to test everything that is available, but some of the pictures you see in this section show the 'before' and 'after' results of our testing the products for 30 days.

As has been said, whatever treatment you choose – and there are many more available – do follow the manufacturers' instructions and stick with their application.

CHAPTER 6
SALON
TREATMENTS

You can't go a beauty salon these days without seeing a menu of anti-cellulite treatments costing anything from £25 to as much as £100 a session. And if you have deep pockets and are desperate enough, you often do want to throw money at the problem.

But do salon treatments actually work? And how much would you need to spend to see results?

Cellulite experts admit that results of salon treatments tend to be short term – popping in for a one-off session isn't going to make a big, lasting difference; all require a long-term course to show any real results. But as part of a three- or four-pronged approach – alongside a healthy diet, regular exercise and an at-home brushing/massage plan, they may give you a boost and kick start your anti-cellulite regime.

What's on offer?

You can usually find a massage-based treatment at your local salon. This manipulation is said to work by increasing your circulation and boosting lymphatic drainage, thereby helping to get rid of the water retention that can give you those bulgy dimples. You are usually massaged with oils or specialist creams, which also help soften your skin.

One session is enough to soften your skin and make your thighs and bottom look a bit smoother, but you'd need regular treatments to make a significant difference. Plus studies have shown that over-vigorous massage can actually cause damage to the lymph system, so opt for manual lymphatic drainage (see page 76) or a gentle massage for best results.

You'll find an increasing number of anti-cellulite therapies which involve the use of electrical devices to massage various firming/toning products into your skin. The idea behind this approach is that the electrical charge is believed to help the products penetrate more deeply. Some use galvanic and isotonic currents, which are said to give the muscle a kind of friction-based 'workout', and thereby help firm up your buttocks/thighs too.

Body wrapping is another cellulite busting mainstay salon treatment. It involves a process of enveloping the cellulite-prone parts of the body with heated blankets, or cling film, or special bandage-style materials. They are used in conjunction with a variety of substances such as herbal extracts, algae, seaweed and mud which are designed to help hydrate the skin, boost circulation and reduce fluid retention. Usually, your skin is brushed or massaged with the products first, and then covered in the wrapping. Some of the wraps work by compressing your thighs tightly, too – and may help you lose inches (largely down to fluid loss) although you need lots of treatments to see lasting results.

Other therapies available are variations on treatments for facial skin such as microdermabrasion. These are said to work by helping to exfoliate, soften and buff the skin, thereby smoothing the orange-peel texture of your thighs. It's claimed they can also help boost the production of new elastin and collagen, so the septae – or collagen fibres – beneath your skin become more elastic and don't squish down those subcutaneous fatty pockets with such unsightly results.

If you're squeamish, and have vast amounts of spare cash, you may have been tempted to try liposuction. This is a medical procedure that involves sucking the fat out of your thighs or stomach or affected areas; apparently it can get rid of as many as 3 litres of fat deposits in one session.

As it's a medical procedure, it carries all the associated risks – so make sure you approach it with your eyes open. You may well lose inches, but there's no evidence that it has any effect on cellulite – and it doesn't focus on the condition of the skin itself. Besides, unless you watch your diet and take regular exercise the fat will come back so, as a cellulite buster, it's not your best option.

Salon treatments to try

Below we've outlined some of the more popular and widely available treatments for cellulite as well as one or two of the more recent 'hybrids'. They may have impressive temporary results, but again they should be used on conjunction with the 30-Day Plan to have a real possibility of making a lasting difference. The consolation is that there's nothing like a salon treatment for making you feel more gorgeous, is there?

MANUAL LYMPHATIC DRAINAGE

What is it? A massage therapy that was developed in the 30s and helps to boost your lymphatic drainage system and circulation, and encourage the filtering of waste and excess fluids from your body. The therapist uses gentle rhythmic pumping techniques to move the skin in the direction of the lymph flow.

How does it work? Think of your lymphatic system like a drainage system, which carries waste products to the lymph nodes. That's where they're processed, then return to the bloodstream where they're sent to the liver to be detoxified – and then excreted. We've seen that a sluggish lymphatic system can cause fluid retention, which is linked with cellulite. Manual lymphatic drainage is considered the best kind of massage treatment for cellulite because it helps to stimulate the lymphatic flow and reduce fluid away from the fatty tissue. It's also gentle; studies have shown violent massage can actually damage the lymph tissue and make the problem worse. Each treatment lasts about an hour and about six to ten are usually recommended.

How much? From about £30 a session. Call 01592 748008 or visit www.mlduk.org.uk.

THALASSOTHERAPY

What is it? It's a water-based therapy (the word *thalassa* means the sea) and it uses sea water and mineral-rich products on the skin. It involves lots of different techniques – from wraps, to baths, to floatation or jets.

How does it work? On two levels. Firstly, water treatments such as thalassotherapy are believed to work by using extremes of temperatures to boost blood circulation. You may, for example, go from a warm water bath to a cold water one. When your circulation works effectively, your organs – including your skin – are provided with the blood and oxygen they need to work at their best. Extremes of heat are also said to help boost your metabolism so this helps process foods and get rid of calories more efficiently.

Secondly, sea water is rich in minerals; these are said to be absorbed into the body so they help rebalance your fluid levels, and 'feed' the skin to help boost healthy collagen production.

Other types of thalassotherapy involve body wraps; products are smeared over your body to help boost the circulation and rebalance fluid levels. You are wrapped in a heat-inducing blanket or bandage wraps to encourage the fluid to be lost. The body-shaping effect is the result of the combined action of perspiration and compression, which leads to a reduction on thighs and buttocks. This effect is mainly due to the loss of fluids and is only temporary. Body wraps are generally lovely and relaxing, and do help soften the skin, but they won't get rid of cellulite alone.

How much? Expect to pay from about £40. For salon details, call Thalgo on 0800 146041 or visit www.thalgo.co.uk.

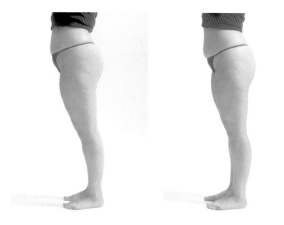

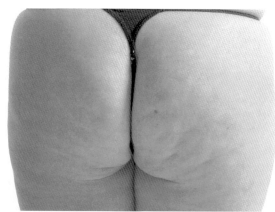

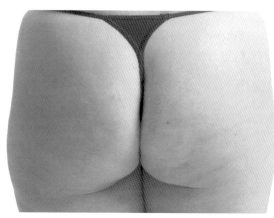

- **Age:** 26
- Diet, exercise and thalassotherapy treatments (6)
- **Total weight loss:** 5 lb (2.3 kg) due to other factors
  – 10 st 10 lb (68.2 kg) to 10 st 5 lb (65.9 kg)
- **Total inch loss:** 4 in (10 cm)

MESOTHERAPY

What is it? Mesotherapy involves injecting small amounts of homeopathic medicine with a small needle immediately beneath the surface of the skin to break down the cellulite and to improve circulation and lymphatic drainage.

How does it work? It's a tailor-made treatment; the remedy administered is combined depending on your own requirements – you may need something to help boost a sluggish circulation, for example. Sometimes vitamin C is included, too, to boost the production of collagen. The process takes about ten minutes. Usually, you are given treatments twice a week over a period of four to eight weeks and then you have top up or maintenance treatments for four to six weeks once a year. Apparently some patients lose up to 2 cm from their thighs after only six sessions, and results can be really effective. But do make sure your practitioner is fully qualified and has some medical training – always check his or her credentials.

How much? Price about £60 a session. Check out www.mesotherapy.co.uk for details.

ENDERMOLOGIE

What is it? A deep machine-massage therapy from France which uses rollers and gentle suctioning to stretch, stimulate and deeply massage the area.

How does it work? One study from Vanderbilt University in the US found that deep mechanical massage can help improve the appearance of cellulite. In this treatment, a machine rolls back and forth across the area and sucks in the skin, loosening and breaking down some of the fat cells, boosting circulation, and stretching the collagen fibres making them more elastic, and spreading the fat into a smooth layer, reducing the lumpy, bumpy appearance.

Results do seem impressive; in the US, the FDA (Food and Drink Administration) approved endermologie as an effective temporary treatment for cellulite. One US study showed that after having seven treatments patients lost about 1.34 cm from their thighs – and these results were effective even if the patients hadn't actually lost weight.

How much? From £70 a session, ten weekly sessions are recommended. It is available in various salons around the country.

MICRODERMABRASION

What is it? It's a skin 'polishing' treatment using machine-applied crystals to buff and smooth the skin. It's used widely for treating stretch marks.

How does it work? Aluminium oxide crystals are designed to flatten and 'polish' the lumps and bumps on your buttocks and thighs. The top layer of skin is exfoliated away, so you are left with smoother, more even-textured skin. It's also said to stimulate the production of new elastin and collagen, which may help prevent the pulling down of the collagen fibres that contributes to the puckering of cellulite areas.

How much? Expect to pay from about £40 (ten sessions are recommended). Call 08705 934 934 for more information.

IONITHERMIE

What is it? This treatment includes a body scrub and pressure point massage; the areas to be treated are covered with thermal clay and essential oils. Then pads, which emit rhythmic electrical pulses, are placed on your skin. This combination of faradic and galvanic stimuli is said to enhance the action of the thermal clay and biologically active natural ingredients.

How does it work? It claims that the application of the therapeutic treatments such as thermal products and essential oils via the electrical currents ensure that their beneficial properties penetrate more deeply. Different currents are said to exercise the muscles, firming them as they go. Ionithermie also claims to help reduce your thighs by up to 8 cm in just one session! Independent studies have shown about ten treatments can improve orange-peel skin.

How much? About £40–50 per session. Five sessions are often recommended. Ionithermie is available throughout the country in prestigious salons and spas. To find out more about the treatments available and where you too can indulge in a pampering ionithermie treatment near your home, simply contact The Skincare Sanctuary on 0800 917 4080.

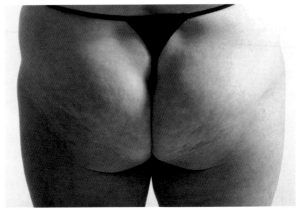

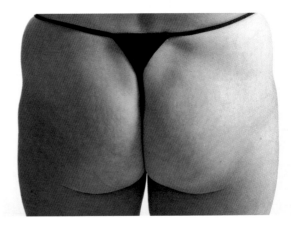

- **Age:** 56
- Took a series of 6 ionithermie treatments, using recommended creams and pills, but did not diet or exercise
- **Total inch loss:** 6 in (15 cm)

FUTUR-TEC SKIN REGENERATOR SYSTEM

What is it? It's an hour-long electrical (but painless) treatment, which combines laser, micro-current, ultrasound and suction.

How does it work? Ultrasound is supposed to dissolve fat cells by blasting them with ultrasound waves. The other currents are said to help firm the skin, stimulate a sluggish lymphatic drainage system, and give your circulation a boost.

How much? From £100 a session, so it's not cheap – plus about eight to ten sessions are recommended. Call 0800 028 7222 for Lasercare Clinics or www.caci-international.com.

AQUA MASSAGE

What is it? You step into a machine similar to that of a sun bed, but fully clothed since there is a layer of plastic separating you from the water. It lasts for about 10 minutes and is completely painless. Normally, the therapist controlling your treatment will send the current of water all over you at the beginning and end of the treatment so that you get used to the sensation.

How does it work? Jets of water are propelled at your body, massaging it and helping to break down the fat deposits under the skin. It also helps to boost circulation. You can choose a special 'Fat Buster' programme, which concentrates on the thighs, hips and buttocks when the water is pummelled at those areas specifically.

How much? It costs from £10 for 10 minutes but you can book courses of four, six or ten treatments for £35, £50 and £80 respectively. Contact Aquazone in Directory of Useful Addresses, page 141.

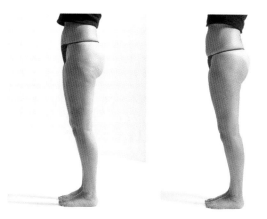

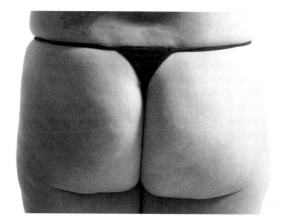

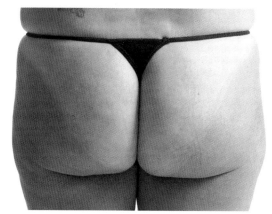

- **Age:** 52
- Took a series of 6 aquamassage treatments, but did not diet or exercise
- **Total inch loss:** 2 in (4 cm)

CHAPTER 7
RECIPES

CARROT SOUP WITH FRESH CORIANDER

MAKES 2 SERVINGS

1 tbsp (15 ml) extra virgin olive oil

1 small onion, finely sliced

1 garlic clove, crushed

4 carrots, sliced

500 ml (16 fl oz) vegetable stock

1 bay leaf

A little low-sodium salt and freshly ground black pepper

A handful of fresh coriander, roughly chopped

Heat the olive oil in a heavy-based saucepan over a moderate heat. Add the onion and sauté gently for about 5 minutes until it is translucent.

Add the garlic and cook for a further 1–2 minutes. Add the carrots, stock and bay leaf to the pan, stir, then bring to the boil. Simmer for 15 minutes or until the vegetables are tender.

Allow the soup to cool slightly for a couple of minutes. Remove and discard the bay leaf. Liquidise the soup using a hand blender or conventional blender. Season to taste with low-sodium salt and pepper, then stir in the fresh coriander.

TOMATO AND VEGETABLE SOUP

MAKES 2 SERVINGS

500 ml (16 fl oz) vegetable stock

300 ml (1/2 pint) passata (smooth sieved tomatoes)

1 onion, chopped

1 garlic clove, crushed

1 carrot, chopped

1 small courgette, trimmed and sliced

60 g (2 oz) fine green beans

60 g (2 oz) frozen peas

60 g (2 oz) frozen broad beans

1 tsp (5 ml) dried basil

1 tbsp (15 ml) extra virgin olive or flaxseed oil

Bring the vegetable stock and passata to the boil in a large saucepan. Add the onion, garlic and carrots. Lower the heat, cover and simmer for 15 minutes.

Add the courgettes, green beans, peas, broad beans and basil, and continue cooking for a further 5 minutes or until the vegetables are tender.

Turn off the heat then stir in the oil. Serve the soup hot in individual bowls.

SPINACH AND COURGETTE SOUP WITH TOASTED ALMONDS

MAKES 2 SERVINGS

1 small onion, finely chopped
1 tbsp (15 ml) extra virgin olive oil
125 g (4 oz) fresh or frozen spinach
225 g (8 oz) courgettes (approx 2)
1 tbsp (15 ml) cornflour blended with a little water
500 ml (16 fl oz) vegetable stock
A little low-sodium salt and freshly ground black pepper
A little grated nutmeg
25 g (1 oz) flaked almonds, toasted under the grill

Cook the onion gently in the olive oil for 5 minutes. Then add the spinach and courgettes, cover and cook for a further 4–5 minutes until the vegetables are tender.

Stir in the cornflour mixture, stirring continuously. When blended, add the vegetable stock. Bring to the boil, stirring, and simmer gently for 1–2 minutes to cook the cornflour.

Put the soup onto a blender with the low-sodium salt, pepper and nutmeg and whiz until smooth.

Ladle the soup into bowls, and sprinkle the flaked almonds over the top of each helping.

CABBAGE, LEEK AND BROCCOLI SOUP

MAKES 2 SERVINGS

1 tbsp (15 ml) extra virgin olive oil
1 onion, finely sliced
1 leek, sliced
125 g (4 oz) cabbage, finely shredded
125 g (4 oz) broccoli florets
1 medium potato, peeled and diced
500 ml (16 fl oz) vegetable stock
A little low-sodium salt and freshly ground black pepper
2 sprigs of fresh parsley to garnish

Heat the olive oil in a heavy-based saucepan over a moderate heat. Add the onion and leek and cook gently for about 5 minutes.

Add the cabbage, broccoli and potato to the pan and mix well. Cook gently over a moderately low heat for a few minutes, stirring occasionally, then add the stock. Bring to the boil, then simmer for 15 minutes or until the vegetables are tender.

Season to taste with low-sodium salt and pepper. To serve, pour into soup bowls and garnish with a sprig of fresh parsley.

PORRIDGE WITH RAISINS AND APRICOTS

MAKES 2 SERVINGS

85 g (2 oz) rolled porridge oats
125ml (4 fl oz) soya, rice, sesame or almond milk
125ml (4 fl oz) water
2 tbsp (30 ml) raisins
8 ready-to-eat apricots
1 tbsp (15 ml) honey

Mix the oats, milk and water in a saucepan. Bring to the boil and simmer for 4–5 minutes, stirring frequently.

Meanwhile, snip the apricots into bite-sized pieces and add them to the cooked porridge along with the raisins.

Spoon into bowls and drizzle the honey on top.

MUESLI WITH FRUIT AND NUTS

MAKES 2 SERVINGS

85 g (3 oz) porridge oats, millet or rice flakes
150 ml (¼ pint) soya, rice, almond or oat 'milk'
2 tbsp (30 ml) raisins or sultanas
2 tbsp (30 ml) toasted flaked almonds or chopped hazelnuts
1 tbsp (15 ml) ground linseeds (optional)
1 apple, peeled and grated or other fresh fruit
(e.g. banana, strawberries)

In a large bowl, mix together the oats (or other flakes), 'milk', dried fruit, nuts and ground linseeds. Cover and leave overnight in the fridge. To serve, stir in the grated apple or other fruit. Spoon into cereal bowls.

FRUIT AND YOGHURT

MAKES 2 SERVINGS

175–225 g (6–8 oz) fresh fruit (e.g. chopped mango, sliced bananas, strawberries, raspberries or blueberries)
300 g (10 oz) soya or natural bio-yoghurt*
1–2 level tbsp (15–30 ml) honey

Place half the fruit in each bowl. Spoon half the yoghurt on top of each bowl. Drizzle with honey.

* Natural dairy yoghurt may be used instead of soya yoghurt if you prefer the taste.

COMPOTE OF DRIED FRUIT

MAKES 2 SERVINGS

300 ml (½ pint) boiling water
150–175 g (5–6 oz) mixed dried fruits
(e.g. figs, apricots, prunes, apples, mangos)
4 tbsp (60 ml) soya or natural bio-yoghurt

Put the dried fruit in a large bowl. Cover with boiling water. Allow to cool, then put covered in the fridge overnight. The fruit should become plump and soft.

Drain the water. Spoon over the yoghurt.

GRILLED AUBERGINES WITH MINT AND YOGHURT DRESSING

MAKES 2 SERVINGS

1 medium aubergine
1–2 tbsp (15–30 ml) olive oil
1 handful fresh mint
Juice of ½ lemon
Freshly ground black pepper
4 tbsp (60 ml) soya or low-fat natural bio-yoghurt
2 tbsp (30 ml) reduced-fat hummus
25g (1 oz) pine nuts

Thickly slice the aubergines into chunky rounds about 1cm (½ inch) thick. Brush a baking sheet with a little of the olive oil and arrange the slices on it in one layer.

Brush the aubergine slices lightly with olive oil and put them under a hot grill. When they are soft and golden and beginning to char at the edges, after about 4–5 minutes, turn them over and cook the other side for 3–4 minutes.

Meanwhile make the dressing: chop the mint quite roughly, and then stir together with 2 tbsp of the olive oil, the lemon juice, black pepper and yoghurt.

Sprinkle the pine nuts over the aubergines and pop back under the grill for 1–2 minutes until toasted. Lift the aubergines off the baking sheet and onto a warmed plate. Spoon the mint and yoghurt dressing over and around the aubergines and serve hot with a dollop of hummus on top.

STIR-FRIED VEGETABLES WITH CASHEWS

MAKES 2 SERVINGS

1 tbsp (15 ml) olive or rapeseed oil
1 small onion, sliced
1 tsp (5 ml) grated fresh ginger
1 garlic clove, crushed
85 g (3 oz) broccoli florets
85 g (3 oz) thin green beans, trimmed
1 courgette, sliced
125 g (4 oz) bean sprouts
1 tbsp (15 ml) water
1 tbsp (15 ml) light soy sauce
60 g (2 oz) cashew nuts, toasted

Heat the rapeseed oil in a non-stick wok or large frying pan. Add the onion, ginger and garlic and stir-fry for 2 minutes. Add the broccoli, green beans and courgette and stir-fry for a further 2–3 minutes. Add the bean sprouts, water and soy sauce, and continue stir-frying for a further minute.

Stir in the cashew nuts and serve.

SPINACH WITH PINE NUTS

MAKES 2 SERVINGS

225 g (8 oz) baby spinach leaves
1 tbsp (15 ml) extra virgin olive oil
60 g (2 oz) pine nuts
1 garlic clove, crushed
Juice of $\frac{1}{2}$ lemon

Put the spinach in a saucepan with 1 tbsp (15 ml) water. Cover and cook over a low heat until the spinach is wilted – about 5 minutes.

Meanwhile, heat the oil in a pan over a gently heat and sauté the pine nuts and garlic until just golden. Stir them into the spinach with the lemon juice. Serve warm.

QUINOA* AND RICE WITH PUMPKIN SEEDS

MAKES 2 SERVINGS

1 tbsp (15 ml) extra virgin olive oil
1 small red onion, chopped
60 g (2 oz) brown rice
60 g (2 oz) quinoa
300 ml ($\frac{1}{2}$ pint) vegetable stock
125g (4 oz) frozen peas
125 g (4 oz) small broccoli florets
4 tbsp (60 ml) pumpkin seeds, lightly toasted
A little low-sodium salt and freshly ground black pepper
Handful of fresh parsley, chopped

Heat the oil in a large saucepan and sauté the onion over a gentle heat for 5 minutes. Add the rice, quinoa and stock and stir well. Bring to the boil, then reduce the heat and simmer for about 20–25 minutes until the liquid has been absorbed and the grains are tender.

Add the peas and broccoli and cook for a further 3–4 minutes.

Stir in the pumpkin seeds. Season with low sodium salt and pepper. Stir in the parsley and serve.

* Available from health food stores. Alternatively, omit this and substitute extra rice.

ROASTED MEDITERRANEAN VEGETABLES WITH OLIVES AND ROSEMARY

MAKES 2 SERVINGS

¹/₂ red pepper, cut into strips
¹/₂ yellow pepper, cut into strips
2 small courgettes, trimmed and thickly sliced
1 small red onion, roughly sliced
¹/₂ aubergine, cut into 2 cm (1 inch) cubes
125 g (4 oz) cherry tomatoes
A few sprigs of rosemary
1 garlic clove, crushed
1–2 tbsp (15–30 ml) extra virgin olive oil
A handful of black olives

Pre-heat the oven to 200°C/400°F/Gas mark 6.

Place all the vegetables in a large roasting tin. Place the rosemary sprigs between the vegetables and scatter over the crushed garlic. Drizzle over the olive oil and toss lightly so that the vegetables are well coated in the oil.

Roast in the oven for about 30 minutes until the vegetables are slightly charred on the outside and tender in the middle. Mix with the black olives.

ROASTED ROOT VEGETABLES

MAKES 2 SERVINGS

2 carrots, peeled and halved
1 parsnip, peeled and cut into quarters
1 medium potato, peeled and sliced
¹/₄ swede, peeled and cut into wedges
¹/₂ small butternut squash, peeled and thickly sliced
1 garlic clove, crushed
A little low-sodium salt and freshly ground black pepper
1–2 tbsp (15–30 ml) olive oil

Pre-heat the oven to 200°C/400°F/ Gas mark 6.

Prepare the vegetables and place in a large roasting tin. Scatter over the crushed garlic, low-sodium salt and black pepper. Drizzle over the oil and turn the vegetables gently so they are coated in a little oil.

Roast in the oven for 30–40 minutes until the vegetables are tender.

SPICED BEANS WITH MUSHROOMS AND SQUASH

MAKES 2 SERVINGS

1 tbsp (30 ml) rapeseed oil
1 onion, chopped
1 garlic clove, crushed
1/2 tsp (2.5 ml) each of ground coriander and ground cumin
1/4 tsp (1.25 ml) turmeric
85 g (3 oz) button mushrooms, halved
1/2 small butternut squash, peeled and diced
200 g (7 oz) tinned chopped tomatoes
400 g (14 oz) can red kidney beans, drained and rinsed
A little low-sodium salt and freshly ground black pepper
A handful of fresh coriander leaves, chopped

Heat the oil in a large pan and add the onions, garlic, ground coriander, cumin and turmeric. Cook over a moderate heat for 3 minutes until the onions have softened.

Add the mushrooms and squash and continue cooking for a further 5 minutes. Add the tomatoes and red kidney beans. Bring to the boil, then reduce the heat and simmer for 10–15 minutes until the vegetables are tender.

Season with the low-sodium salt and pepper. Stir in the fresh coriander just before serving.

CHICK PEAS WITH SPINACH AND POTATO

MAKES 2 SERVINGS

1 tbsp (15 ml) extra virgin olive oil
1 onion, chopped
1 garlic clove, crushed
1 red pepper, deseeded and chopped
2 medium potatoes, peeled and cut into 2 cm (1 inch) chunks
400 g (14 oz) tinned chopped tomatoes
250 ml (8 fl oz) vegetable stock
400 g (14 oz) tinned chick peas, drained and rinsed
175 g (6 oz) fresh spinach, washed and trimmed

Heat the oil in a heavy-based pan, add the onion, garlic and red pepper, and cook over a moderate heat for 5 minutes.

Add the potatoes, tinned tomatoes, vegetable stock and chickpeas, stir then bring to the boil. Lower the heat and simmer for 20 minutes, stirring occasionally.

Stir in the spinach, cover and continue cooking for a few minutes until the spinach is wilted. Serve in individual bowls.

LENTIL DAHL WITH FRESH CORIANDER

MAKES 4 SERVINGS

1–2 tbsp (15–30 ml) olive oil
1 onion, chopped
1 garlic clove, crushed
½ tsp (2.5 ml) ground cumin
1 tsp (5 ml) ground coriander
85 g (3 oz) red lentils
400 ml (12 fl oz) vegetable stock
2 small carrots, diced
125 g (4 oz) frozen peas
1 tbsp (15 ml) lemon juice
A little low-sodium salt
A small handful of fresh coriander, finely chopped

Heat the oil in a heavy-based pan and sauté the onions for 5 minutes. Add the garlic and spices and continue cooking for 1 minute.

Add the lentils, stock and carrots. Bring to the boil. Cover and simmer for about 20 minutes, adding the peas 5 minutes before the end of the cooking time.

Stir in the lemon juice and low-sodium salt. Finally, stir in the fresh coriander.

CRUDITÉS

Florets of broccoli
Florets of cauliflower
Strips of red, yellow, orange or green pepper
Carrot sticks
Celery sticks
Small mushrooms
Cherry tomatoes
Crisp chicory leaves
Mangetout
Baby sweetcorn
Radishes
Spring onions
Cucumber, cut into strips
Courgette, cut into strips

HUMMUS

MAKES 4 SERVINGS
400 g (14 oz) tinned chickpeas
2 garlic cloves, crushed
2 tbsp (30 ml) extra virgin olive oil
120 ml (4 fl oz) tahini (sesame seed paste)
Juice of 1 lemon
2–4 tbsp (30–60 ml) water
A little low-sodium salt and freshly ground black pepper
Pinch of paprika or cayenne pepper

Drain and rinse the chickpeas. Put them in a food processor or blender with the remaining ingredients, apart from the paprika. Process to a smooth paste. Add extra water if necessary to give the desired consistency. Adjust the seasoning to taste.

Spoon into a serving dish. Pour over a little olive oil and sprinkle with cayenne or paprika. Chill in the fridge for at least 2 hours before serving.

GUACAMOLE

MAKES 4 SERVINGS
2 ripe avocados
2 tbsp (30 ml) lemon or lime juice
½ small red onion, finely chopped
1 garlic clove, crushed
2 tomatoes, skinned and chopped
2 tbsp (30 ml) fresh coriander, finely chopped
Sea salt and freshly ground black pepper

Halve each avocado; remove the stone and scoop out the flesh. Mash the avocado flesh with the lemon or lime juice, using a fork. Add the remaining ingredients, mixing well.

Check the seasoning, adding a little more black pepper or lemon juice if necessary. Spoon into a serving dish, cover and chill.

ROMAINE SALAD WITH HONEY AND MUSTARD DRESSING

MAKES 2 SERVINGS

1 romaine lettuce
½ cucumber, thinly sliced
1 red pepper, sliced
2 tomatoes, quartered
A handful of flat leaf parsley or mint
1 ripe avocado
1 tbsp (15 ml) lemon juice

DRESSING

2 tbsp (30 ml) extra-virgin olive oil
1 tbsp (15 ml) cider vinegar
¼ tsp (1.25 ml) Dijon mustard
½ level tsp (2.5 ml) clear honey
½ clove of garlic

Cut the lettuce leaves into 1 cm (½ inch) pieces and place them in a large bowl. Add the cucumber, peppers, tomatoes and herbs.

Halve, peel and pit the avocado. Cut into 0.5 cm (¼ inch) slices and place in a small bowl. Toss in the lemon juice to prevent discoloration. Add the avocado to the salad.

Place the dressing ingredients in a bottle or screw-top glass jar and shake together. Pour over the salad and toss well.

SPINACH, ROCKET AND AVOCADO SALAD

MAKES 2 SERVINGS

85 g (3 oz) baby spinach leaves
85 g (3 oz) rocket
1 avocado
1 small courgette
2 tbsp (30 ml) extra virgin olive oil
1 tbsp (15 ml) lemon juice
1 garlic clove, finely chopped

Place the spinach and rocket in a large bowl. Cut the avocado into quarters, remove the stone and then peel carefully. Slice lengthways. Trim and thinly slice the courgette. Combine the salad leaves, avocado and courgettes.

Shake the olive oil, lemon juice and garlic in a bottle or screw-top glass jar; then drizzle over the salad. Toss lightly then serve.

FLAGEOLET BEAN SALAD WITH PEANUTS

MAKES 2 SERVINGS

200g (7 oz) canned flageolet beans, rinsed and drained
¼ cucumber
2 tomatoes
2 tbsp (30 ml) chopped fresh parsley
1 tbsp (15 ml) pumpkin-seed oil*
1 tbsp (15 ml) extra virgin olive oil
1 tbsp (15 ml) cider vinegar
2 tbsp (30 ml) peanuts

Place the beans in a large bowl. Dice the cucumber and tomatoes. Add to the beans along with the parsley and combine well.

Shake the pumpkin-seed oil, olive oil and vinegar in a bottle or screw-top glass jar and drizzle over the salad. Toss. Scatter over the peanuts.

* Alternatively substitute extra olive oil.

WARM CHICKPEA SALAD WITH GREEN BEANS AND CASHEWS

MAKES 2 SERVINGS

125 g (4 oz) thin green beans, trimmed
200 g (7 oz) can chickpeas, drained and rinsed
60 g (2 oz) cashew nuts, lightly toasted
1 tbsp (15 ml) fresh parsley, chopped
1 packet (100 g) of ready-washed watercress

DRESSING

2 tbsp (30 ml) extra virgin olive oil
1 tbsp (15 ml) balsamic vinegar
1 small garlic clove, crushed
½ tsp (2.5 ml) Dijon mustard

Steam the beans for 4 minutes until they are tender-crisp. Drain then refresh under cold running water. Place in a large bowl and combine with the chickpeas, cashews and parsley.

Place the dressing ingredients in a bottle or screw-topped glass jar and shake until combined. Add half of the dressing to the chickpea salad and mix until well combined.

Place the watercress in a bowl and toss with the remaining dressing. Spoon the chickpea salad over the watercress.

RICE NOODLES WITH VEGETABLES IN SPICED COCONUT MILK

MAKES 2 SERVINGS

85 g (3 oz) rice noodles
1 tbsp (5 ml) olive oil
1 small onion, chopped
1 garlic clove, finely chopped
½ tsp (2.5 ml) grated fresh ginger
1 tsp (5 ml) ground coriander
Pinch of ground turmeric
200 ml (7 fl oz) coconut milk
125 ml (4 fl oz) vegetable stock
85 g (3 oz) green beans
125 g (4 oz) green cabbage, shredded
Small handful of fresh coriander, chopped

Cook the noodles according to the instructions on the packet. Drain.

Heat the oil in a wok or large saucepan. Add the onion, garlic, ginger, ground coriander and turmeric and stir-fry for a few minutes. Add the coconut milk and stock and bring to the boil. Reduce the heat and stir in the green beans, cabbage and cooked noodles. Cover and simmer for 5 minutes.

Stir in the coriander and serve in individual bowls.

PASTA WITH SPRING VEGETABLES

MAKES 4 SERVINGS

2 tbsp (30 ml) extra virgin olive oil
1 garlic clove, crushed
3–4 shallots, chopped
125 g (4 oz) mangetout, trimmed
125 g (4 oz) asparagus, trimmed and cut into 5 cm (2 inch) lengths
125 g (4 oz) baby spinach leaves
350 g (12 oz) non-wheat pasta shapes
A small handful of fresh mint leaves, chopped
A little low-sodium salt and freshly ground black pepper

Heat the olive oil in a pan and cook the garlic and shallots for 3 minutes until softened.

Steam or boil the vegetables in a minimal quantity of water for 3–4 minutes until tender-crisp. Drain immediately.

Meanwhile, cook the pasta in boiling water according to the packet instructions. Drain then combine with the cooked vegetables and shallot mixture.

Add the mint and season with low-sodium salt and pepper. Toss well and serve immediately.

PASTA SPIRALS WITH GRILLED VEGETABLES

MAKES 2 SERVINGS

½ red pepper, cut into wide strips
½ yellow pepper, cut into wide strips
1 small courgette, thinly sliced lengthways
1 small red onion, thinly sliced
4 tomatoes, halved
Extra virgin olive oil, for brushing
175 g (6 oz) non-wheat pasta spirals
Handful of fresh basil leaves

Preheat the grill to high. Arrange the pepper strips, courgettes, onion and tomato halves in a single layer on a grill pan. Brush with a little olive oil and grill for 2 minutes on each side.

Meanwhile, cook the pasta in boiling water according to the packet instructions. Drain then combine with the cooked vegetables mixture.

Scatter over the basil leaves.

SALAD LEAVES WITH FRESH HERBS AND WALNUTS

MAKES 2 SERVINGS

1 pack (85 g) of ready-washed salad leaves
1 handful of fresh herbs (e.g. coriander, parsley, basil, mint)
60 g (2 oz) walnut halves, lightly toasted
1 tbsp (15 ml) extra virgin olive oil
1 tbsp (15 ml) walnut oil
1 tbsp (15 ml) lemon juice

Place the salad leaves and herbs in a large salad bowl. Add the walnuts.

Place the extra virgin olive oil, walnut oil and lemon juice in a bottle or screw-top jar and shake together thoroughly. Pour over the salad leaves, then toss so that every leaf is well coated with the dressing. Serve immediately.

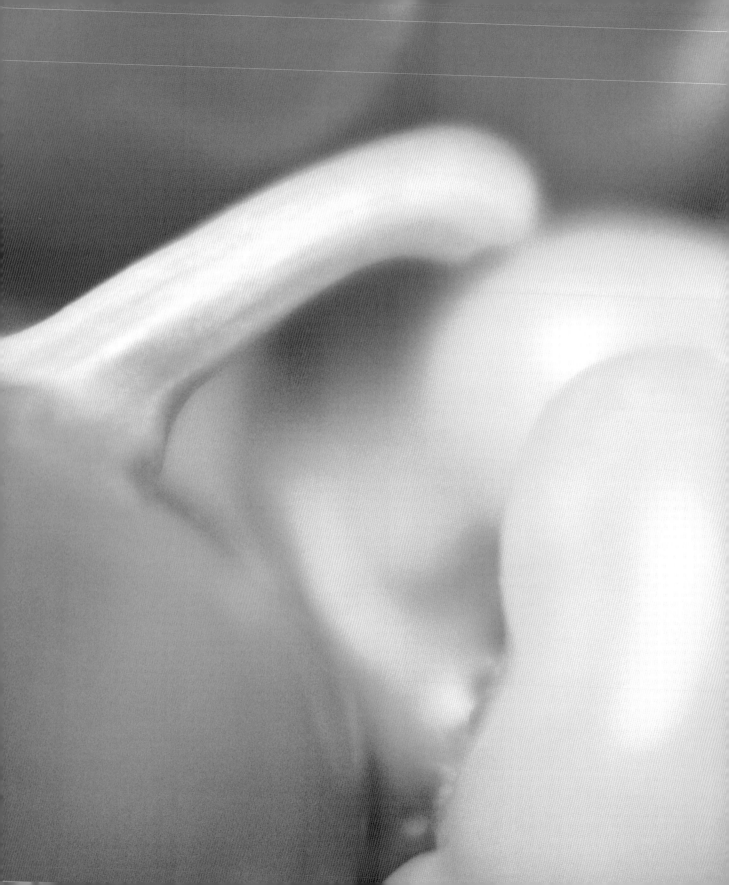

PENNE WITH RATATOUILLE

MAKES 2 SERVINGS

2 tbsp (30 ml) extra virgin olive oil

1 onion, peeled and chopped

1/2 each of red, yellow and green peppers, deseeded and sliced

1 garlic clove, crushed

1/2 aubergine, diced

2 small courgettes, sliced

400 g (14 oz) can tomatoes

A little low sodium salt and freshly ground black pepper

175 g (6 oz) non-wheat penne pasta

2 tbsp (30 ml) chopped fresh parsley

Heat the oil in a large saucepan. Add the onions and peppers and cook gently for 5 minutes. Add the garlic, aubergines, courgettes and tomatoes. Stir, then cover and cook over a low heat for 20–25 minutes until all the vegetables are tender. Season to taste with salt and freshly ground black pepper and sprinkle with the chopped parsley.

Meanwhile, cook the pasta in boiling water according to the packet instructions. Drain, then combine with the ratatouille.

NOODLE AND TOFU STIR FRY

MAKES 2 SERVINGS

Juice of 1 lime (or lemon)

2 tbsp (30 ml) water

2 garlic cloves, crushed

175g (6 oz) firm tofu, cubed

85 g (3oz) rice noodles

1 tbsp (15 ml) olive or sesame oil

2.5 cm (1 inch) piece fresh ginger, chopped

4 spring onions, chopped

225g (8 oz) mushrooms, sliced

125g (4 oz) bean sprouts

1 tsp (5 ml) cornflour

Mix the lime (or lemon) juice, water and half the garlic in a small shallow dish. Add the tofu, stir to coat in the marinade and set aside for 30 minutes.

Cook the noodles in a saucepan according to the instructions on the packet. Drain.

Heat the oil in a wok and stir-fry the remaining garlic and ginger for 1 minute. Add the spring onions, mushrooms and bean sprouts, and stir-fry for 2 minutes. Add the drained noodles and cook a further minute.

Drain the tofu, reserving the marinade and add to the vegetables and noodles. Blend the reserved marinade with the cornflour to make a smooth paste, then pour over the vegetables. Continue cooking, stirring constantly until the sauce has thickened. Transfer onto a serving dish.

FRESH FRUIT WITH HONEY

MAKES 2 SERVINGS

4 tbsp (60 ml) hot water
1 tbsp (15 ml) acacia (or clear) honey
1 banana, peeled and sliced
175 g (6 oz) berry fruits (e.g. strawberries, raspberries, blueberries)
2 kiwi fruit, peeled, cut into 1 cm (½ inch) pieces
125 g (4 oz) seedless grapes

Dissolve the honey in the hot water in large bowl. Prepare the berry fruit, slicing into bite-sized pieces, if necessary. Add all the fruit to the honey syrup in the bowl. Toss to combine. Cover and chill until you are ready to serve.

RASPBERRY TOFU CREAM

MAKES 2 SERVINGS

225 g (8 oz) raspberries
150 g (5 oz) silken tofu
½ tsp (2.5 ml) vanilla extract
1 level tbsp (15 ml) clear honey
A few extra raspberries

Place the raspberries in a blender or food processor with tofu, vanilla extract and honey. Blend until smooth.

Decorate with a few whole raspberries. Chill in the fridge and serve.

TROPICAL FRUIT SALAD WITH HONEY AND LIME

MAKES 2 SERVINGS

½ papaya (pawpaw)
½ mango
¼ fresh pineapple (or approx 4 rings of tinned pineapple)
1 lime
2 tsp (10 ml) clear acacia honey
30 g (1 oz) flaked toasted almonds

Cut the papaya and mango flesh into cubes. Cut the pineapple into four 1 cm (½ inch) rounds, then cut each round into quarters. Place the fruit in a large bowl.

Finely grate the rind from the lime and add to the fruit. Squeeze the juice and pour into a small saucepan with the acacia honey. Heat gently, stirring, just until the honey has dissolved. Allow to cool.

Pour the lime syrup over the fruit and toss well. Scatter over the flaked toasted almonds.

WARM BERRY COMPOTE WITH CINNAMON

MAKES 2 SERVINGS

225 g (8 oz) mixed fresh or frozen berries (e.g. raspberries, blackberries, strawberries, cranberries, blueberries)
2 tbsp (30 ml) honey
1 cinnamon stick
2 slices orange

Put the fruit into a saucepan and add the honey, cinnamon stick and orange slices. Add just enough water to cover. Bring to the boil, then reduce the heat and simmer, stirring from time to time for 10 minutes until the liquid has reduced by half.

Allow to cool, then remove the cinnamon stick and orange slices.

FRUIT JELLY

MAKES 2 SERVINGS

1 level tbsp (15 ml) agar agar flakes (or 1 sachet gelatine)
300 ml (½ pint) red or purple grape juice
250 g (9 oz) fresh or frozen berry fruit (e.g. strawberries, raspberries, blueberries)

Mix together the agar agar (or gelatine) and grape juice in a small saucepan. Bring to the boil, whisking continuously; reduce the heat and simmer for 4–5 minutes. Allow to cool.

Place the fruit in a large bowl (or two individual bowls) and pour the cooled liquid jelly over to cover the fruit.

Chill in the fridge for 1–2 hours until set.

SMOOTHIES

MANGO AND ORANGE SMOOTHIE

MAKES 2 DRINKS

200 ml (7 fl oz) orange juice
1 mango, skinned, stone removed and chopped
1 banana, cut into chunks
A cupful of crushed ice

Place the orange juice, mango, banana and ice cubes in the goblet of a smoothie maker, blender or food processor, and blend for about 45 seconds until smooth. Serve immediately.

STRAWBERRY AND BLUEBERRY SMOOTHIE

MAKES 2 DRINKS

125 g (4 oz) strawberries, hulled
125 g (4 oz) blueberries
1 small banana, peeled and cut into chunks
125 ml (4 fl oz) fresh orange juice
A cupful of crushed ice

Place the ingredients in a smoothie maker, blender or food processor, and blend until smooth and frothy. Serve immediately.

MELON AND PEACH SMOOTHIE

MAKES 2 DRINKS

¹/₄ medium cantaloupe melon, peeled, seeded and chopped
1 peach, skinned, stoned and chopped
1 small banana, peeled and cut into chunks
A cupful of crushed ice

Blend the ingredients together in a smoothie maker, blender or food processor and blend until frothy and smooth. Serve immediately.

STRAWBERRY SMOOTHIE

MAKES 2 DRINKS

250 ml (8 fl oz) orange juice
175 g (6 oz) strawberries
1 banana, peeled and cut into chunks
A cupful of crushed ice

Place the orange juice, strawberries, banana and crushed ice in a smoothie maker, blender or food processor, and blend until smooth and thick. Serve immediately.

PINEAPPLE, MANGO AND COCONUT SMOOTHIE

MAKES 2 DRINKS

¹/₂ pineapple
1 mango, skinned, stone removed and chopped
125 ml (5 fl oz) coconut milk
1 banana
150 ml (5 fl oz) pineapple juice
A cupful of crushed ice

Place the ingredients in a smoothie maker, blender or food processor and blend until smooth. Serve immediately.

CHAPTER 8
EXERCISES

In the introduction to the 30-Day Plan, you will have found some basic details about the exercise programme. This section contains the details of which exercises should be completed on which days. Although, we have recommended a weekly pattern starting on a Monday, you can easily adjust it to suit your own starting day.

You will also find a breakdown of which exercises are suitable for each section of the body and full instructions for all the stretches and exercises. Remember: this is not a race. You must adapt the routine to fit in with your lifestyle.

SPOTTY DOGS

With a gentle jump up, stride forward with one leg while taking the other leg back (the stride distance need not be large) in an open-scissors motion, remembering not to allow your knee to go too far forward.

Repeat, with the other leg forward.

Once you have mastered this action, introduce the arms, either by taking both arms forward and back together or alternating them with the opposite leg.

Repeat this action for 2–4 minutes.

The exercises are as follows:

Stretches

Adductors stretch
(inner thigh muscles)

Bicep stretch (front of
arm and chest muscles)

Deltoid stretch
(shoulder muscles)

Leg/Gluteal (buttocks) stretch
(front of leg and bottom muscles)

Back stretch (back and
abdominal muscles)

Tricep stretch
(back of arm muscles)

Upper Body

Press-up (chest, shoulder
and tricep muscles)

Hand-climbs (shoulder, back
and chest muscles)

Tricep dips (back of arm muscles)

Dumbbell shoulder press
(palms in) (shoulder muscles)

Breast stroke (chest and arm
muscles)

Seated bicep curl (front
of arm muscles)

Middle Body

Static abdominals

Diagonal crunches

Leg V-sit

Each lower body stretch should be held for 30 seconds after every lower body exercise. Likewise, each upper body stretch should be held for 30 seconds after every upper body exercise. The middle body exercises should all be followed with the back/abdominal stretch, held for 30 seconds.

It is proven that it is more productive to carry out exercises for a period of time rather than completing sets of repetitions, so we recommend that each exercise be performed for a period of 20 seconds for the first week, increasing by 10 seconds each week. It is not necessary to carry out all four sections on a daily basis – they will be split into groups as shown on the following pages.

Lower Body

Wall squat-thrusts (leg and bottom muscles)

Sprint toe run (all leg and bottom muscles)

Jumping squat (front of leg and bottom muscles)

Hamstring curl (back of leg and bottom muscles)

Pulsing squat (front of leg and bottom muscles)

Reverse lunge (inner-/outer-thigh and bottom muscles)

WEEK ONE

Monday   Lower body plus complementary stretches
Tuesday   Upper body, middle body plus complementary stretches
Wednesday   Lower body, middle body plus complementary stretches
Thursday   Upper body plus complementary stretches
Friday   Lower body, middle body plus complementary stretches

Each exercise within the groups above (i.e. lower body, middle body and upper body) should be performed continuously for 20 seconds. Use 2 kg hand weights or dumbbells for upper body exercises. After each exercise, the complementary stretch should be held for 30 seconds.

WEEK TWO

Monday	Lower body plus complementary stretches
Tuesday	Upper body, middle body plus complementary stretches
Wednesday	Lower body, middle body plus complementary stretches
Thursday	Upper body plus complementary stretches
Friday	Lower body, middle body plus complementary stretches

Each exercise within the groups above (i.e. lower body, middle body and upper body) should be performed continuously for 30 seconds. Use 2 kg hand weights or dumbbells for upper body exercises. After each exercise, the complementary stretch will be held for 30 seconds.

WEEK THREE

Monday	Lower body plus complementary stretches
Tuesday	Upper body, middle body plus complementary stretches
Wednesday	Lower body, middle body plus complementary stretches
Thursday	Upper body plus complementary stretches
Friday	Lower body, middle body plus complementary stretches

Each exercise within the groups above (i.e. lower body, middle body and upper body) should be performed continuously for 40 seconds and incorporate the use of ankle weights for the lower body exercises. Use 3 kg hand weights or dumbbells for upper body exercises. After each exercise, the complementary stretch should be held for 30 seconds.

WEEK FOUR

Monday   Lower body plus complementary stretches
Tuesday   Upper body, middle body plus complementary stretches
Wednesday   Lower body, middle body plus complementary stretches
Thursday   Upper body plus complementary stretches
Friday   Lower body, middle body plus complementary stretches

Each exercise within the groups above (i.e. lower body, middle body and upper body) should be performed continuously for 50 seconds and incorporate the use of ankle weights for the lower body exercises. Use 3 kg hand weights or dumbbells for upper body exercises. After each exercise, the complementary stretch should be held for 30 seconds.

STRETCHES

ADDUCTOR STRETCH

Sit on the floor with the soles of your feet placed together and your hands placed around your ankles or lower legs, keeping your back straight and your shoulders back.

Direct your knees towards the floor.

Apply pressure with your elbows to your inner thigh (adductor) muscles.

BICEP/CHEST STRETCH

Place an outstretched straight arm with open palm against a wall or tree (if outside).

Slowly turn your body away, keeping the palm firmly in contact with the wall (or tree).

DELTOID STRETCH

Take one arm across the front of your body and use the other arm to pull the elbow joint towards the chest.

LEG/GLUTEAL (BUTTOCK) STRETCH

Sit on the floor with either leg out straight and the opposite leg crossed over at the knee joint (foot flat on the floor, next to the knee of the outstretched leg).

Using the opposite elbow, pull the bent leg across towards the body.

Simply reverse the arms and legs to stretch the other side.

BACK STRETCH

Lie on your back with your knees bent, feet flat on the floor and arms out to the sides at shoulder level.

Rotate your knees to one side lowering them towards the floor as far as is comfortable.

N.B. Keep the upper body grounded.

TRICEP STRETCH

Place one arm behind your head with your hand directed down your spine.

Take your other hand over your head, applying pressure to the elbow joint while stretching the tricep.

Simply reverse arms to stretch the opposite side.

UPPER BODY EXERCISES
PRESS-UP

Lie on the floor on your front with your hands beside your shoulders.

Push yourself up, straightening your arms and keeping your back straight.

Then lower your body by bending at the elbows, but don't let your body touch the floor.

If a full press-up cannot be managed, modify the exercise by putting your knees on the floor rather than your feet. Avoid putting your bottom in the air and arching your back.

HAND CLIMBS

Using a bottom stair or heavy box (approx. 24 cm high), position your body in a press-up stance with your palms on the floor in front of the step or box. If you cannot manage a full press-up stance, then put your knees on the floor rather than your feet.

Take one hand at a time to the top of the step before returning to the starting position.

Aim to keep your back parallel to the floor throughout the exercise by pushing off from your feet (or knees, as shown here in the modified version) while keeping your toes in the same position.

TRICEP DIPS

Sit on a steady chair (put the back of the chair against a wall to secure it if necessary) and place your hands on the front edge of the seat.

Move your bottom forward off the seat and lower your body so your arms are bent at the elbow at a 90° angle.

Push back up until your arms are straight and repeat.

Keep your legs bent at the knee and point your toes upwards. Make sure your bottom is kept close to the edge of the chair for maximum effect.

DUMBBELL SHOULDER PRESS (PALMS IN)

Either standing or sitting, hold a pair of dumbbells at shoulder height with palms facing inwards.

Raise the dumbbells above your head.

Inhale as you lift, and exhale as you lower the weight back down to shoulder level.

UPPER BODY EXERCISES

BREAST STROKE

Hold the dumbbells at chest level in front of the body.

Make a smooth circular motion (i.e. as if swimming breast stroke style), aiming to keep the weights up and your back straight.

SEATED BICEP CURL

Sit on a chair holding a dumbbell in either hand aiming to keep your wrist tilted inwards.

Lower your arm from the elbow out straight and then curl, folding your forearm upwards.

MIDDLE BODY EXERCISES
STATIC ABDOMINALS

Resting on your forearms, and your toes, hold your body up.

Ensure your elbows are under your shoulder blades with your forearms facing forwards.

Move forwards over your hands, bending your arms at the elbows.

Aim to maintain a straight line throughout your legs and back.

Lie on your back.

Place your right arm flat on the floor at a right angle to your body.

Keep your right shoulder firmly rooted to the floor.

Place the outer edge of your right foot on your left knee.

With your left hand placed at the side of your head, move the left elbow diagonally to the right knee.

Repeat by alternating sides.

LEG V-SIT

Lying on your back with arms straight above your head on the floor, keep one foot flat on the floor while raising the other leg towards your middle.

At the same time, raise your hands up to touch the foot.

You can support your neck by placing one hand behind your head.

LOWER BODY EXERCISES
WALL SQUAT THRUSTS

Stand in front of a wall (or tree, if outside) and place your palms flat on the wall, with your arms stretched out straight.

Raise alternate knees towards the chest in a rapid, continuous movement.

SPRINT TOE RUN

With your hands clasped in front of you and your feet shoulder-width apart, staying nimble on your toes, rapidly alternate lifting and lowering your feet a few inches from the floor.

This can be completed in an upright position or a lowered squatting position.

JUMPING SQUAT

Maintaining the squatting position, with your hands clasped in front of your body, jump laterally a few inches forwards then backwards continuously.

N.B. Do not let your knees go over your toes.

HAMSTRING CURL

Stand with your feet shoulder-width apart, knees slightly bent.

Bring alternate heels up towards your bottom.

Transfer your body weight to the foot that is grounded, leaning slightly to the side to keep your balance.

Repeat on the other leg in a continuous motion.

PULSING SQUAT

Resume the squatting position.

Place your hands outstretched in front of you (to aid balance).

Pulse up and down approximately 10 inches without resuming a full standing position or a full squatting position.

Do this continuously.

REVERSE LUNGE

Place your feet together and your hands on your hips.

Control your legs as you extend one leg forwards to the lunge position.

Make sure your knees do not bend more than 90°.

Push off with the front leg, keeping your upper body straight, and raise the front leg off the floor.

Drop it by the other foot and repeat the exercise using the opposite leg.

DIRECTORY OF USEFUL ADDRESSES

The following list of salons and health spas that offer treatments which help combat cellulite is by no means comprehensive, so it is always worth asking friends or checking out those listed in your local telephone directory. However, the information below may prove a helpful starting point should you wish to try out a salon treatment.

For details of salons in your area which offer ionithermie, please contact:
The Skin Sanctuary on 0800 917 4080

LONDON AND SOUTH EAST

AESTHETIC BEAUTY CENTRES
70 High Street, Broadstairs, Kent CT10 1JT
Tel: 01843 866833

5 THE COLONNADE
Broadway Centre, Maidstone, Kent ME6 8PS
Tel: 01622 679 9222
Website: www.abcbeauty.co.uk/endermologie.htm
Endermologie, Microdermabrasion

AESTHETIC AND LASER CLINIC
Gravesend Medical Centre, 1 New Swan Yard,
Gravesend, Kent DA11 2EN
Tel: 01474 534 123
Website: www.kentlaser.co.uk
Mesotherapy, Microdermabrasion

AMIDA TOTAL WELLBEING
The Racquets and Fitness Spa, Stanhope Grove
Beckenham, Kent BR3 3HL
Tel: 020 8662 6160 / Fax: 020 8658 1535
Website: www.amidaclubs.com
Ionithermie, Furtur-Tec, Manual Lymphatic Drainage

BALLIFSCOURT HOTEL AND HEALTH SPA
Climping, Nr Arundel, West Sussex BN17 5RW
Tel: 01903 723 511 / Fax: 01903 723 107
Email: bailiffscourt@hshotels.co.uk
Website: www.hshotels.co.uk
Manual Lymphatic Drainage

BAY TREE MAISON
The Old Station House, 175 Dukes Ride
Crowthorne Berkshire RG45 6NZ
Tel: 01344 750 751
Website: www.baytreemaison.com
Thalassotherapy, Ionithermie

BOSTON CLINIC (UK) LTD
63a Moscow Road, Bayswater, London W2 4JS.
Tel: 020 7229 3904
Website: www.boston-clinic.co.uk
Mesotherapy, Microdermabrasion

CHAMPNEYS
Forest Mere, Liphook, Hampshire GU30 7JQ

Henlow Grange, Henlow, Bedfordshire SG16 6DB
Tel: 08703 300 300
Website: www.Champneys.com
Thalassotherapy, Manual Lymphatic Drainage

ELAN HEALTH AND BEAUTY CENTRE
38a High Street, Rayleigh, Essex SS6 7EF
Tel: 01268 770 660
Email: info@elan-beauty.co.uk
Website: www.elan-beauty.co.uk
Mesotherapy

GRACE HEALTH AND BEAUTY
Clanfield Farm House, Clanfield, Oxfordshire PO8 0RA
Tel:02392 599199 / Fax:02392 618 310
Manual Lymphatic Drainage

HURLINGHAM CLINIC AND SPA
67 Studdridge Street, London SW6 3TD
Tel: +44 (0) 20 7348 6380 / Fax: +44 (0) 20 7348 6388
Email: info@hurlinghamclinic.com
Website: www.hurlinghamclinic.com
Endermologie

MEDICO BEAUTY NURSE SERVICES
South Lodge, Wexham Street, Wexham
Nr Slough SL2 4HS
Tel: 01753 554980

MEDICO BEAUTY NURSE SERVICES
57 North Street, Thame, Oxfordshire OX9 3BH
Tel: 01844 213007
Website: mbnsclinic.co.uk
Endermologie, Mesotherapy

NUTFIELD PRIORY
Nutfield, Redhill, Surrey RH1 4EL
Tel: 01737 824 400 / Fax: 01737 823 321
Email: nutpriory@aol.com
Website: www.nutfield-priory.com
Manual Lymphatic Drainage

SHRUBLAND HALL HEALTH CLINIC
Codenham, Ipswich, Suffolk IP6 9QH
Tel: 01473 830404 / Fax: 01473 832641
Website: www.shrublandhall.co.uk
Futur-Tec (CACI)

THE BODY CLINIC
10 Harley Street, London W1G 9PF
Tel: 0845 601 1962
Email: mailto:infor@thebodyclinic.co.uk
Web: www.thebodyclinic.co.uk
Endermologie

THE CHELSEA CLUB SPA
Chelsea Village, Fulham Road, London SW6 1HS
Tel: 0 20 7915 2215 / Fax: 0 20 7915 2214
Website: www.chelseaclub.com
Endermologie

THE DORCHESTER HOTEL
Park Lane, London W1A 2HJ
Tel: +44 (0) 20 7629 8888 / Fax: +44 (0) 20 7409 0114
Email: cfisher@dorchesterhotel.com
Website: www.dorchesterhotel.com
Manual Lymphatic Drainage, Thalassotherapy

THE GRAND HOTEL EASTBOURNE
King Edwards Parade, Eastbourne, East Sussex
BN21 4EQ
Tel: 01323 412 345 / Fax: 01323 412 233
Email: reservations@grandeastbourne.com
Website: www.grandeastbourne.com
Manual Lymphatic Drainage

THE WIMPOLE SKIN CARE CENTRE
Suite 1, 55 Wimpole Street, London W1G 8YL
London: 0207 487 5465
Virginia Water: 01344 842 953
Weybridge: 01932 253730
Walton-On-Thames: 01932 253730
www.amidaclubs.com
Website: www.wimpoleskincare.com
**Microdermabrasion, Endermologie,
Mesotherapy**

VIRGIN SPAS
London, Acton 0208 6009 638
London, Islington 0207 0149 745
London, Wandsworth 0208 704 0445
Website:www.virgincosmetics.com
Futur-Tec

UTOPIA SPA AT ROWHILL GRANGE HOTEL
Wilmington, Nr Dartford, Kent DA2 7QH
Tel: 01322 667 433 / Fax: 01322 615 137
Email: mailto:admin@rowhillgrange
Website: www.rowhillgrange.com
Ionithermie

SOUTH WEST

AQUA ZONE
2nd Floor, Debenhams, 1–5 St James Barton, Bristol
BS99 7JX
Tel: 0117 9272 272
Website: www.theaquazone.com
Aquamassage

BUDOCK VEAN HOTEL
Nr Helford Passage, Mawnan Smith, Falmouth,
Cornwall TR11 5LG
Tel: 01326 252 100 / Fax: 01326 250 892
Email: relax@budockvean.co.uk
Website: www.budockvean.co.uk
Lymphatic Drainage Massage

CHEWTON GLEN HOTEL SPAN
AND COUNTRY CLUB
New Milton, Hampshire BH25 6QS
Tel: 01425 275341
Website: www.chewtonglen.com
Thalassotherapy

LUCKNAM PARK
Colerne, Chippenham, Wiltshire SN14 8AZ
Tel: 01225 742 777 / Fax: 01225 743 536
Email: reservations@lucknampark.co.uk
Website: www.lucknampark.co.uk
Lymphatic Drainage Massage

THE BATH SPA HOTEL
Sydney Road, Bath BA2 6JF
Tel: 0870 400 8222 or 01225 444424 / Fax: 01225 444006
Email: sales@bathspahotel.com
Website: www.bathspahotel.com
Detoxifying Drainage Massage

TYLNEY HALL HOTEL
Rotherwick, Hook, Hampshire RG27 9AZ
Tel: 01256 764 881 / Fax: 01256 768 141
Email: reservations@tylneyhall.co.uk
Website: www.tylneyhall.co.uk
Manual Lymphatic Drainage

MIDLANDS

CHAMPNEYS SPRINGS
Packington, Ashby-de-la-Zouch, Leicestershire
Tel: 08703 300 300
Website: www.healthfarms.co.uk/resort_springs.asp
Thalassotherapy

EDEN HALL DAY SPA
Elston Village, Newark, Nottinghamshire NG23 5PG
Tel: 01636 525 555 / Fax: 01636 525 185
Email: info@edenhallspa.co.uk
Website: www.edenhallspa.co.uk
Body Contouring Body Wraps

HEALTH DU VIN
Hotel Du Vin, Church Street, Birmingham B2 2NR
Tel: 0121 200 0600 /Fax: 0121 236 0889
Email: info@birmingham.hotelduvin.com
Website: hotelduvin.com
Lymphatic Drainage Massage

NORTH EAST

ALDWARK MANOR
Nr Alne, North Yorkshire YO61 1UF
Tel: 01347 838 146 / Fax: 01347 838 867
Email: aldwark@marstonhotels.com
Website: www.marstonhotels.com
Lymphatic Drainage Massage

LINDEN HALL
Longhorsley, Morpeth, Northumberland NE65 8XF
Tel: 01670 500 000 / Fax: 01670 500 001
Email: mailto:stay@lindenhall.co.uk
Website: www.lindenhall.co.uk
Lymphatic Drainage Massage

THE SERENITY SPA AT SEAHAM HALL
Lord Byron's Walk, Seaham, County Durham SR7 7AG
Tel: 0191 516 1550 / Fax: 0191 516 1413
Email: info@seaham-serenityspa.com
Website: www.seaham-serenityspa.com
Endermologie

THORPE PARK HOTEL & SPA
1150 Century Way, Thorpe Park, Leeds, Yorkshire LS15 8ZB
Tel: 0113 264 1000 / Fax: 0113 264 1010
Email: thorpepark@shirehotels.co.uk
Website: www.spa.thorpeparkhotel.co.uk
Lymphatic Drainage Massage

NORTH WEST

ARMATHWAITE HALL HOTEL
Bassenthwaite Lake, Keswick, Cumbria CA12 4RE
Tel: 017687 76551 / Fax: 017687 76220
Email: reservations@armathwaite-hall.com
Website: www.armathwaite-hall.com
Manual Lymphatic Drainage, Endermologie

COSMOPOLITAN SPIRIT – BEAUTY SPA
19 Brown Street, Manchester M2 1DA
Tel: 0161 834 7690 / Website: HYPERLINK
Website: www.cosmopolitanspirit.co.uk
Microdermabrasion

THE CHESTER CRABWELL MANOR
Parkgate Road, Mollington, Chester, Cheshire CH1 6NE
Tel: 01244 851 666 / Fax: 01244 851 400
Email: crabwallmanor@marstonhotels.com
Website: www.marstonhotels.com
Lymphatic Drainage Massage, Microdermabrasion

SCOTLAND

CRIEFF HYDRO HOTEL
Crieff PH7 3LQ
Tel: 01764 655 555
Email: enquiries@crieffhydro.com
Website: www.crieffhydro.com
Endermologie

OSHI SPA AT LANGS HOTEL
2 Port Dundas Place, Glasgow, Lanarkshire G2 3LD
Tel: 0141 333 5701 / Fax: 0141 333 5700
Website: www.langshotels.co.uk
Lymphatic Drainage Massage

STOBO CASTLE HEALTH SPA
Stobo, Peeblesshire EH45 8NY
Tel: 01721 760249 / Fax: 01721 760294
Reservations: 01721 760600/Treatments: 01721 760344
Email: reservations@stobocastle.co.uk
Website: www.stobocastle.co.uk
Hydromassage, Lymphatic Drainage Massage, Ionothermie

NORTHERN IRELAND

ELYSIUM SPA
Culloden Hotel, Bangor Road, Holywood, Belfast, Co. Down BT18 0EX
Tel: 028 9042 1066 / Fax: 028 9042 6777
Email: elysium@cull.hastingshotels.com
Website: www.hastingshotels.com
Lymphatic Drainage Massage

IMPRESSIONS
Health and Beauty Clinic, Burrendale Hotel, 51 Castlewellan Road
Newcastle, Co. Down BT33 0JY
Tel: 028 4372 4448
Email: reservations@burrendale.com
Futur-tec, Lymphatic Drainage Massage, Hydromassage

WALES

ST. DAVID'S HOTEL & SPA
Havannah Street, Cardiff Bay, Cardifff, South Glamorgan CF10 5SD
Tel: 02920 454045 / Fax: 02920 487056
Email: thestdavidshotel@rfhotels.com
Lymphatic Drainage Massage, Hydromassage

THE CELTIC MANOR RESORT HOTEL
Coldra Woods, Newport, Gwent NP18 1HQ
Tel: 01633 413 000 / Fax: 01633 412 910
Email: postbox@celtic-manor.com
Hydromassage

CHANNEL ISLANDS

DE VERE GRAND HOTEL ESPLANADE
St Helier, Jersey JE4 8WD
Tel: 0870 606 3606 / Fax: 01925 403020
Email: crsreservations@devere.co.uk
Brochure Hotline Service: 01925 639499
Thalassotherapy

REPUBLIC OF IRELAND

BODY BENEFITS (AESTHETIC SKINCARE & LASER CLINIC)
13/14 The Cornstore, St Augustine Street, Galway, Co. Galway
Tel: +353 (0) 91 567 500 / Fax: +353 (0) 91 567 520
Email: clinics@bodybenefits.ie
Website: www.bodybenefits.biz
Endermologie

GALWAY BAY HEALTH FARM
Loughaunrone House, Oranmore, Co. Galway
Tel: +353 (0) 91 790606 / Fax: +353 (0) 91 790837
Email: lochan@iol.ie
Website: www.galwaybayhealthfarm.ie
Hydromassage

KILKEE THALASSOTHERAPY CENTRE
Grattan Street, Kilkee, Co. Clare
Tel: 065 905 6742 / Fax: 065 905 6762
Email: mulcahype@eircom.net
Website: www.kilkeethalasso.com
Thalassotherapy

POWERSCOURT SPRINGS HEALTH FARM
Coolakay, Enniskerry, Co. Wicklow
Tel: +353 (0) 1 276 1000 / Fax: +353 (0) 1 276 1626
Email: info@powerscoursprings.iol.ie
Website: www.powerscourtsprings.ie
Lymphatic Drainage Massage, Massage Therapy

CAROL'S WEBSITES AND HER FAVOURITE PRODUCTS

Do you want to buy the best products? Do you want more information about the detox and cellulite solution? Do you, perhaps, want to take part in some trials for products for the face and body, and eating and exercise plans in the future (don't worry, bottom shots are not compulsory)?

Well, in January 2005, new websites are being launched.
www.carolvorderman.net
www.carol-vorderman.com

These will contain all sorts of extra information for you, plus the chance to take part in future trials. You'll be able to e-mail me with your thoughts and results so that we can constantly improve what we have to offer. Put the website names in your list of favourites on your computer.

As the websites develop, we'll be launching some new creams and lotions for the face and body (I'm really excited about this as they've been getting great results on trial), and you'll be able to buy my favourite products and receive newsletters with all the latest information.

Over the last few years, I've experimented with hundreds of products and foods in a quest to find the very best. I've also received thousands and thousands of e-mails and letters from men and women who have tried my Detox plan and found it has changed their lives for the better. I know that once you've completed the Cellulite Plan and seen how it's made a difference to you, you'll want to know more.

If you aren't linked up to the Internet, then don't worry: we will also be operating a direct mail order business.

To find out more, just write to
Carol Vorderman Mail Order
P.O. Box 200, Bristol BS20 7WX

Or e-mail: john@johnmiles.org.uk
Or Fax: 01275 810186

BOOKS

Detox For Life – the 28-Day plan
£10.99 First published 2001
This is the detox bible, a bestseller which has altered the lives of thousands of people. Follow the detox plan and weight loss and energy are guaranteed.

The Summer Detox 14-Day plan
£10.99 First published 2003
The summer detox was devised especially for those who want to lose pounds to get into a new bikini. The recipes use summer foods specifically so that you can benefit as much as possible in a short space of time.

Detox Recipes
£11.99 First published 2003
This beautiful cookery book shows just how exciting and tasty detox recipes can be. It includes dishes for the strict detoxer and those on a maintenance plan and has proved to be the ideal companion to the books above. This would help anyone following the Cellulite 30-Day plan.

SIMPLY ORGANIC 'IDEAL FOR DETOX' READY MEALS

In 2003 I tried a ready meal I'd bought in a supermarket made by a small company called Simply Organic. It tasted amazing, there were no additives and every ingredient was organically grown. It was also very handy because, as usual, I didn't have time to prepare a meal for one. As a lot of detoxers need to take food to work with them or have busy lives when they too don't have time to cook, I thought it would be great to work with Simply Organic to produce an 'Ideal For Detox' range. The range was launched in late 2003 and is now available in most of the big supermarkets in the UK. It includes soups and ready meals and all of the range is suitable for anybody using the Cellulite 30-Day plan.

Ideal For Detox Chunky Vegetable Soup
A really tasty veggie soup. Eat it alone, or with an oatcake or rye bread.

Ideal for Detox Lentil and Parsley Soup
This soup is really thick and gorgeous and perfect for autumn and winter days. It'll fill you up for the rest of the day.

Ideal For Detox Mixed Bean Chilli
A wonderful chilli, there's a lot of it in the dish so if you finish it, you're doing well. If you want to eat it in the evening with brown rice and salad, even better. It's very filling and you won't need any pudding afterwards.

Ideal For Detox Lentil and Winter Vegetable Stew
This dish is full of slow releasing energy. Eat it alone, or with brown rice or rye bread.

Ideal For Detox Morroccan Vegetable Tagine
With a tangy tomato base this vegetable tagine is delicious

INDEX